"I highly recommend this book to teens everywhere. Suzi covers topics that are current and relevant with students. Her writing style is easy to read and makes you feel like you are sitting down having a conversation with her. The practical advice she gives in this book is timeless and if followed, will help teens grow in their relationship with God."

—ROB MCCLURE
Oklahoma District Youth Director,
Oklahoma Youth Ministries

"This book will strengthen your trust muscle and open you up to God's activity in all areas of life. If you're looking for a cute read, this book is not for you. If you're looking for something to ignite your faith, start reading now! I'm constantly on the lookout for resources that take God's Word seriously and that trust teens to be up for the challenge. This book does just that."

—BARRY SHAFER
Founder and director, InWord Resources
Middletown, Ohio

"*Making It Real* will engage you and take you on a faith-building and life-changing journey, leading you daily to a powerful one-on-one encounter with God. This book connects our generation with a message that is relevant, inspiring, and desperately needed."

—BEAU HEBERT
President, YouthFire.com

"*Making It Real* will help teens examine and nurture their faith no matter where they are in their spiritual journey. Simple to read but powerful in its impact, *Making It Real* will change lives."

—SARAH ANNE SUMPOLEC
Author of the teen-fiction series Becoming Beka

"*Making It Real* provides teens with the necessary tools to make smart choices in life. Through engaging stories and in-depth devotions, Suzanne covers life issues that all teens face."

—HEATHER JAMISON
Author, *Real Stuff: A Survivor's Guide*

"If you are struggling with questions about your faith, direction for your life, issues of trust, or compromising morals, this book will help you ask honest questions—and even more important, you'll find honest answers. With frank advice, compelling stories, and tender concern, T. Suzanne Eller helps you get real with yourself and real with God."

—ALICE GRAY
Best-selling author, *Stories for a Teen's Heart* and *Small Acts of Grace*

"If you've ever wanted a training manual for making your faith-walk relevant on a day-to-day basis, here it is! Suzanne's book, *Making It Real: Whose Life Is It Anyway?*, will challenge you to know what's true, then live it. You've got to read it. Really."

—ANDREA STEPHENS
Author, *Girlfriend, You Are a B.A.B.E.!:
Beautiful, Accepted, Blessed, Eternally Significant*
Founder of the B.A.B.E. Seminars for teen girls

Making It Real

Making It Real

Whose Faith Is It Anyway?

T. Suzanne Eller

Kregel
Publications

Making It Real: Whose Faith Is It Anyway?

© 2007 by T. Suzanne Eller

Published by Kregel Publications, a division of Kregel, Inc., P.O. Box 2607, Grand Rapids, MI 49501.

Library of Congress Cataloging-in-Publication Data
Eller, T. Suzanne.
  Making it real : whose faith is it anyway? / by T. Suzanne Eller.
     p.   cm.
  1. Teenagers—Religious life. 2. Faith. 3. Devotional literature. I. Title.
BV4531.3.E45 2007
248.8'3—dc22   2006033682

ISBN 10: 0-8254-2543-3
ISBN 13: 978-0-8254-2543-1

Printed in the United States of America

07 08 09 10 11 / 5 4 3 2 1

To Josh Hall.
We watched as you struggled to
grasp the love of Jesus.
You showed what God can do
in a hungry heart.
Who knew that one day you would
be one of our own?
Welcome to the
Eller family.

Contents

Part 4: Destiny: What Does God Want from Me?

Acknowledgments

I want to thank all the teens at M1A who have called me "Mama Suzie." I love you and you inspire me with your faith and your relationships with God.

I appreciate the encouragement of my family: Richard, Leslie, Ryan, Melissa, and Josh. You rock!

Thank you to Janet Grant, my agent and cheerleader.

Thank you to Kregel for hearing my heartbeat for this generation.

Last, I will never forget meeting God for the very first time and how that encounter changed my life. I will run after him all my days with a grateful heart.

Introduction

Have you ever asked yourself questions like: Why can't I feel God? What do I really believe? Is there more to my faith than this?

If you have, you are not alone. Even the disciples—guys called to hard-core ministry—wrestled with these questions. They encountered Jesus, and their lives were turned upside down; but that encounter was just the beginning of their faith walk. As they followed Jesus their lives were marked by destiny, but also became more complicated. They saw miracles happen right in front of them, but they also witnessed people rejecting their message. They preached to people hungry for truth, but encountered religious people acting anything but godly. They sat at Jesus' feet as he taught them, then were persecuted for those same beliefs. The more time they spent with Jesus, the more they grasped real-life answers . . . and also stumbled onto more questions.

It's no different today. Faith is a simple concept, but it is also complex. What you hear from your pastor may be vastly different than what you hear from unbelieving friends. You live out your convictions in a world that doesn't always understand them. In the midst of this complexity, you might find yourself trying to sort out what is truth and what is hype. This leads to important questions that every follower of Christ should pause to ask. The cool thing is that God has already provided answers.

> Jesus told them, "This is what God wants you to do: Believe in the one he has sent." (John 6:29 NLT)

What does God want from you? He wants you to believe in him.

Move in close because I want to share a secret. God is more than a Sunday-school-carbon-copy-faraway God. Real faith is intimate faith. It's more than going to church and warming a pew. Knowing God means that you encounter him for yourself and base your belief system on that discovery.

But I go to church!

I hear you and that's awesome, but I'm not referring to hanging out with the youth group or signing up for the next activity, trip, or fine-arts event. These are all very good things, but knowing God isn't limited to a building or to activities. According to Isaiah, God is so much bigger than any building or event!

> This is what God the LORD says—
> he who created the heavens and stretched them out,
> who spread out the earth and all that comes
>   out of it,
> who gives breath to its people,
>   and life to those who walk on it.
>
> (Isa. 42:5 NIV)

Do you want to find your unique and special relationship with the God of the universe? Over the next few weeks, you'll discover what it means to walk with Christ as a modern-day disciple. You'll answer questions and dig into devos designed to kick-start your faith to an alive, intimate relationship with an amazing God, whether you've known about him your whole life or just figured it out last week. You'll scrape away the outer trappings of your belief system to discover the four *D*'s:

1. Which way do I go? That's *direction.*
2. What do I believe? That's *decision.*
3. Who do I trust? That's *dilemma.*
4. What does God want from me? That's *destiny.*

Throughout the chapter you'll encounter "Into Me See" questions. I have redefined intimacy to "Into Me See" because you'll take off the mask and give God a backstage pass. You might feel spiritually exposed as you allow him to see your heart and thoughts and doubts.

> But for you who welcome him, in whom he dwells—even though you still experience all the limitations of sin—you yourself experience life on God's terms. (Rom. 8:10)

But get this! No matter what lurks there, God isn't afraid of it. As long as you are truthful, then you're going to grow spiritually. Honesty is a tool that God can work with. And this is the benefit: you experience life on God's terms!

——————————— Part 1

DIRECTION

Which Way Do I Go?

Ripping Myself in Two

I'm trying to get out of this place
With my feet stuck to the floor
I'm in this filth that's all around me
And I want a part of it no more

I'm tearing myself apart
Drawing the line in the sand
I'm ripping myself in two
I'm becoming a new man

It's hard to leave this behind
It's what I've always known
But God knows I'll try
I can't do it on my own.

—Barron Bebee, age 19

1

Detours and Shortcuts

[REAL QUOTE]

I miss the time when I was a little girl and I just believed. Now it's filled with explanations and doubt and trying to get rid of the doubt. For some reason, a long time ago, it stopped being simple. I just want it to be about me and God.

—Amanda W., age 17

I glanced at the digital compass in the car. I was driving in the right direction, but nothing looked familiar. I checked the gas gauge; I had less than an eighth of a tank. It was almost dark and wouldn't be long before I was smack out of gas and stuck in a creepy jungle of dirt roads, low-hanging trees, and twisting roads.

It all started when I tried to take a shortcut. I was a city girl, and one wrong turn on the country road twisted me deep into nothingness. My sense of direction was quickly out of whack. I was about to despair when I saw headlights in the distance. I focused on the swishing lights and twisted and turned the car down dirt roads until I found the highway.

When I pulled out onto the asphalt, I realized that I was never completely lost. I had just temporarily lost my bearings.

Sometimes the same thing happens in a person's faith life. You're rocking along, comfortable with hanging out with the youth group, dunking for Spam and playing other gross food games, and showing up for Sunday services. This is the map to your faith life. It's comfy and familiar. It works as long as you stay in the groove.

But what happens when life slips you a detour and you land in unfamiliar territory? Sometimes you lose your bearings.

That's what happened to Erin.

Erin barely had time to come home from college to see her friends or family, much less to go to church. University life was awesome! There were new friends to meet and things to do 24/7. Living as a college freshman was everything she thought it would be, and more!

Erin's mother had hinted for three weeks that she'd like Erin to attend youth service. She even promised to cook lasagna and garlic cheese bread. It was a bribe and Erin knew it, but it was a tantalizing offer, especially after six weeks of cafeteria food.

When Erin walked into the Saturday night youth service, the room was pitch black. A large screen flickered at the front. She was crawling over people to find a seat and stopped, mesmerized by the video that splashed to life in front of her. It was a scene from youth camp the summer before. The camera zoomed in on Erin and her friends standing in front of the altar. Erin was crying, but smiling through her tears. Her eyes were closed. There was a look of pure peace on her face.

As Erin watched herself on screen, she prayed the lights would stay down long enough to get it under control. She swiped away the tears that threatened to fall. She remembered how she had felt that night. She had experienced God in a whole new way. The words she saw herself whispering on the screen were promises that she made to God. The same promises she forgot just weeks into college.

Erin slipped out of the youth service. She pushed open the double doors and fled to her car. She punched in the numbers of her mom's cell, grateful when voice mail picked up instead of her mom.

"Hey, Mom, something came up. Catch you next time, okay? I love you."

Erin pulled into traffic and as she drove back to school, thoughts bumped around in her brain like the tires spinning on the asphalt below her. She tried to remember the last time she spent a moment alone with God. Somehow in the hustle and busyness of college, spiritual intimacy had waltzed into the past, along with her high school yearbook and youth group friends.

At college, there were new experiences, new temptations, and new friends to fill the void. When she saw herself on the screen, she understood that she left something valuable behind in her new journey. Erin began that night to look for the swishing lights to help her find her way back.

HEART CHECK

Don't wait to figure out the truth about your faith.

Let's explore the wrong turns that caused Erin to lose her bearings.

Wrong Turn 1: Living by Feelings

At camp, Erin was in a no-television, no-cell phone, no-temptation zone. Her experiences with God were genuine and made her desire to be with him even more. But when she left home for college, distractions and temptations hit full force. Life was busy. College was awesome and exhausting. There were things to do, and hanging out with God wasn't on the schedule. Soon her faith became a distant memory, kind of like that sweatshirt you crammed under your bed last week. You know it's there if you need it, but for right now it's fine where it is.

Erin dug down deep to find the reasons why she should say

no to temptation, but came up empty. Church and God seemed too far away and the people who usually kept her on track were nowhere in sight.

It wasn't the first time that feelings dictated Erin's belief system. In high school, her faith life was like a bungee cord, bouncing from high to low. If she had a spectacular experience, her faith blazed like a firecracker. If she didn't feel God, her faith fizzled and popped. Living by feelings robbed her of a consistent faith walk.

Making It Real

You know that you are living your faith life by feelings when God is only as great or as small as your last experience. This is roller coaster Christianity at its finest. You experience God and you swoosh up. You make a mistake and you plummet. You don't worship God in service or in your daily life because you feel unworthy.

When your faith is all about feelings, it's easy to nosedive. The real danger of living your faith by feelings is that when you no longer feel God, you might be tempted to turn to what feels good at the moment.

This is the scoop: God is bigger than your feelings.

> I pray that you will begin to understand the incredible greatness of his power for us who believe him. This is the same mighty power that raised Christ from the dead and seated him in the place of honor at God's right hand in the heavenly realms. (Eph. 1:19–20 NLT)

Who is that power for? You and me. You've already read it once, but it's worth repeating. God is searching for someone to believe in him. When you place your trust in feelings, you believe in your emotions or circumstances rather than scriptural truth.

Let's say that you messed up big time. You're standing in a

Sunday night service and everybody knows what happened. If you allow opinions or your shame to keep you from worshipping God, then you've made God as small as your feelings. Think about this. Why not worship Christ because he's the only one who can put you back on track? When you get real with him and ask him to forgive you, you find answers that help you make a better choice next time. Your faith becomes more about God than about you.

Many believers limit their one-on-ones with God to camp or really great church services, but that makes it tough to keep the relationship tight. It's like tuning into your best friend once every few weeks or so. The relationship is still there; it's just not as close as it could be.

Even when you are doing everything "right," sometimes you'll have to deal with feelings, like maybe a best friend moves away, or your mom and dad go through hard times. But no matter what happens, God's love for you remains firm. He's always on the scene and his power is available to you. He will walk with you through the tough times.

INTO ME SEE

Do I live my faith by feelings?

Wrong Turn 2: Living on Borrowed Convictions

In high school Erin had a check and balance system in place. If she strayed too far, a talk with her mom or youth pastor brought her back into the safety zone. In college she was flying solo in her faith life. She believed in God and accepted the Bible as truth, but those beliefs weren't necessarily hers. Her convictions came from sermons, her parents' example, and her Christian upbringing. In her old environment, many of her friends and Erin had the same views about the hot topics of the day. If you asked Erin about her opinion on any given subject from relationships to sex to war, she shared what she had been taught.

At college she was challenged on her principles at every turn. Erin often struggled to define why and what she believed. Like looking through a kaleidoscope, her perspective and convictions got all jumbled up.

Making It Real

You know that you are living on borrowed convictions if you've never taken the time to explore your convictions for yourself. What does the Bible really say about the issues?

> But for right now, friends, I'm completely frustrated by your unspiritual dealings with each other and with God. You're acting like infants in relation to Christ, capable of nothing much more than nursing at the breast. Well, then, I'll nurse you since you don't seem capable of anything more. (1 Cor. 3:1–2)

When babies are born, their digestive system can't handle solid food. If you give an infant green beans before his stomach is ready, everybody suffers later. That period of physical immaturity lasts only a few months. Soon he's ready to graduate from a milk-only diet to mushy cereal and pureed green beans and then solid food, and then one day he's chewing on steak!

A lot of Christians keep a bib tucked under their chins and drink spiritual milk even after they're full-grown. They sit in the pew or in a Sunday school class and open their mouths like baby birds. Feed me! Feed me! That may seem like a funny image, but it's closer to the truth than many will admit.

This is the truth: the Bible rocks! Like a movie, you get to see the beginning and ending of real-life stories like Matthew the tax collector who finds out there's more to life than money, or Peter, the guy nobody believed in, who went on to be a revolutionary of the New Testament.

When the youth pastor reads a Scripture, do you check it out for yourself? If your spiritual diet consists of Scripture verses tossed out like worms from the beaks of others, you miss out on the depth of the Word of God. If you expect your parents or others to supply the core of your convictions, you'll stand on a slippery slope when you come face to face with those who oppose (or don't understand) your beliefs. If you don't know why you believe, how do you expect others to get it?

Wrong Turn 3: Confusing Faith with Tradition

A tradition is something that you do by habit or custom. If you have Christmas at your grandparents' house every year or unwrap gifts on Christmas Eve only, that's a family tradition or custom.

For Erin, church was a part of her life. She had heard a thousand sermons. She grew up watching Veggie Tales and singing "I Love My Lips" along with Larry the Cucumber.

Making It Real

When you are raised in church, you have more than the basics down. You understand the concept of grace, how to share your faith, how to lead and serve, but at some point you have to sort through what is personal and what is tradition.

> I'm after love that lasts, not more religion.
> I want you to know God, not go to more
> prayer meetings.
> (Hos. 6:6)

Going to church on Sunday is an amazing freedom. It's a temple where like-minded believers freely come to worship God. It's a house of prayer. It's a place of healing. It's a place where you can study God's Word together.

It's a community of believers.

Let's dive deeper. Jesus lives inside of you and *you* are a temple. When you worship God on a daily basis you offer him love that lasts rather than religion. You grasp his healing power when you ask God to move in when you feel broken. You add to your faith when you get alone with him and search his Word. By making God more than a habit, you learn what it means to call yourself Christian. No one can strip your faith away because it's deeper than rituals or habit.

Wrong Turn 4: Making Faith a Group Activity

When Erin no longer had church services or Sunday dinners with her family, she felt a little bit lost. She needed music, hype, and people in order to worship God.

> And I pray that Christ will be more and more at home in your hearts as you trust in him. May your roots go down deep into the soil of God's marvelous love. And may you have the power to understand, as all God's people should, how wide, how long, how high, and how deep his love really is. (Eph. 3:17–18 NLT)

HEART CHECK

A personal relationship with God is first a singular activity.

Can you imagine dating a guy or girl, but never taking the time to know them outside the group? If you spend all your time together hanging out with friends, what happens when it's time to walk down the aisle? And what happens the day after that? What about the next year? How do you work together as a team to face good and bad times? What do you talk about?

Spending time with your church friends is scriptural. You find strength as you worship together, but have you devoted time to God as well?

Making It Real

Your faith is a group activity when you avoid one-on-ones with God or wait for the music to tell you when and how to respond to him. The physical building you call church isn't the only place to find God. He's available to you outside those four walls. Spending daily time with God is where your real walk begins.

U-Turn

When Erin left the church that night, she asked herself hard questions. Over time she found the answers she was looking for. Erin built a solid foundation of faith based on a personal relationship with God. Her faith and traditions didn't look exactly like her mom or dad's, but she owned them. She knew exactly who Jesus Christ was and what he meant to her. Erin was definitely out of her comfort zone at times, but the girl on the screen—the one making promises to God, the one in love with her Savior—matched the girl who walked in faith every day.

Have you uncovered the real reason you call yourself a Christian? Do you rely on hand-me-down faith or a set of directions and rules clunking around in your head, but not your heart?

Over the next five days, you'll continue the process of carving out your own faith. Dig into the Word. Be transparent as you answer the questions. Don't beat yourself up if the answers are less than what you hoped for. You'll be one step closer to finding the headlights swishing in the distance.

Crucial Question: Is God More Than a Feeling?
Real Scripture: Acts 16:19–34

A guy named Paul was doing everything right when his world came crashing down. He introduced a fortuneteller to God. She was a slave and her owners weren't too excited that she was hanging an "out of business" sign. They were all about the money, so they seized Paul and Silas and hauled them before the authorities. Paul and Silas were stripped and severely beaten and thrown in jail.

> Along about midnight, Paul and Silas were at prayer and singing a robust hymn to God. The other prisoners couldn't believe their ears. (Acts 16:25)

Paul is naked and battered, but the dude is singing like he's trying out for the choir. Instead of being angry at God, Paul was singing because his faith wasn't based on feelings or circumstances. He believed that God would work it all out for his good.

It's hard when circumstances throw you down like a beefy WWF wrestler. It's difficult when you don't feel God and you desperately want to. But your feelings, or lack of them, don't mean that God isn't in the picture. Stand on truth rather than emotion.

Making It Real

Think about this:

- God is faithful when you are searching to believe.
- God is strong when you are weak.
- God is consistent when you stumble.
- God is forgiving when you make a mistake.

God knows "the rest of the story." He can bring good from the harsh events we encounter; in fact, it's his specialty.

When Paul was singing, it intrigued the jailer so much that he gave his life to God. Paul didn't know the outcome when he began singing, but God was on the scene.

What does this story teach you about trusting God rather than your feelings?

Talking with God

God, you're bigger than my feelings. Today I choose to trust in you rather than react and live by my emotions and feelings. I want consistent faith.

Crucial Question: Do I Own My Convictions?
Real Scripture: Acts 6:8–15

No one gets in your face when you're hiding your passion for God, but when you start living out your convictions, it's a different story. Stephen was full of faith and wisdom. He had the courage of a warrior. When Stephen prayed for people, cool things happened.

> Now Stephen, a man full of God's grace and power, did great wonders and miraculous signs among the people. (Acts 6:8 NIV)

Some religious people were angry and decided that a good old-fashioned debate was in order. Every time they threw out an argument, Stephen spoke with wisdom. Some said he had the face of an angel when he talked. The debate made the religious people look foolish, so they started rumors about Stephen, and he was hauled to court.

When he was accused, Stephen shared his convictions. It was the most eloquent speech of his day.

Making It Real

Right now there are believers in more than sixty nations who suffer persecution. Not just words or name calling, but hunger, beatings, prison, and even death. Why do they suffer? Because of their convictions. When asked to reject their faith, they can't because they believe and are willing, like Stephen, to die.

Have you given much thought to your convictions? Ask God to reinforce and strengthen your core belief system as you search his Word for truth that you can apply to your life.

Talking with God

Dear Lord, take me to the next level. Open my heart to hear your Word and understand. God, teach me how to live out my convictions with courage, wisdom, and faith.

Crucial Question: Is My Faith More Than a Habit?
Real Scripture: 1 Samuel 1:9–17; 2:12–17

Scott is a PK—preacher's kid. Sometimes that's a tough gig because you are expected to live a perfect life, even though you're no different than anyone else. When Scott was fifteen, he wrestled with the PK title. He loved his parents, but church sometimes felt like a burden until one day he figured out that God was the only one he needed to please. Then he became a GK—God's kid.

Samuel was also raised in the church. His mother, Hannah, wanted a baby more than anything. A priest named Eli prayed for her, and little Samuel was born. When he was still a child, Hannah brought her son to the church, hoping that the priest and his family would help her son grow up to know God.

But there was one problem. Eli's sons were wicked. Sure, they performed all the right rituals and traditions, but they also abused their position of power. God was sad and angry because these brothers were disrespectful to their faith and to him. Faith and the priesthood had become so common to these PK's—priest's kids—that they took them for granted.

> Now Samuel did not yet know the LORD: The word of the LORD had not yet been revealed to him. (1 Sam. 3:7 NIV)

Eli and his sons were given an opportunity to introduce young Samuel to God, but how could they when their faith was little more than a habit?

Making It Real

The church is the body of Christ, and it's nearly two thousand years old. It is an army of children, teenagers, men, and women of all ages, races, and languages from all over the world. The church is you and me, and it's the guy in North Korea who is in chains for his faith. When you look at the church in that light, it's so much more than tradition. It's God's kingdom and it's made up of human beings marked with purpose.

Do you see the bigger picture?

If going to church has been a habit, are you willing to step up and offer yourself as a team player in the kingdom of God?

Samuel and the sons of Eli were raised in the same church, but had two very different experiences. What was the difference?

_____

_____

_____

Talking with God

Heavenly Father, thank you for the community of believers in my life. Thank you for the fun times and the teaching and my friends in my local church, but help me not to make my faith a habit. Help me to find my place in your kingdom.

DEVO DAY 4

Crucial Question: Is My Faith Only a Group Activity?
Real Scripture: Exodus 33:7–23

The job description could have read: Wanted! A person to lead thousands of grumbling people out of slavery and into the desert. Patience required!

Leadership was a job that Moses didn't apply for, but a position to which God appointed him. Moses was a child of Hebrew slaves. His mother, in an attempt to save his life from an evil king, floated him down the river. He was rescued and adopted by Pharaoh's family.

Later, his true identity was revealed and it was decision time: Moses could live as an imposter or choose his true identity.

He started his new job as the leader of a massive nation. As he led thousands through the wilderness, Moses pitched a tent outside camp. It was called the Tent of Meeting. The routine went like this:

> When Moses would go to the Tent, all the people would stand at attention; each man would take his position at the entrance to his tent with his eyes on Moses until he entered the Tent; whenever Moses entered the Tent, the Pillar of Cloud descended to the entrance to the Tent and GOD spoke with Moses. All the people would see the Pillar of Cloud at the entrance to the Tent, stand at attention, and then bow down in worship, each man at the entrance to his tent. (Exod. 33:7–10)

When Moses entered the tent, the Israelites hung back with the crowd and watched as the glory of God descended.

Making It Real

How often do you get alone with God in your own Tent of Meeting? Or do you hang back with the crowd and watch as others experience the presence of God? Do you want to be a friend of God? That relationship develops in the one-on-ones. Are there things (thoughts, issues, doubts) that you wish you could talk to God about? Perhaps today is a good day to begin. Find a place where you can unplug and get alone with God. Don't worry about what you should say, just be real with him.

Is intimacy reserved only for preachers or leaders or "perfect" people?

_____

_____

_____

Talking with God

Dear Lord, I don't want my faith to be a spectator sport. I don't want to be hanging with the crowd watching you from a distance. Today I'll choose my own Tent of Meeting and spend time with you. Thank you for the wisdom and maturity that I'll find face-to-face with you every day.

DEVO DAY 5

Crucial Question: Am I Ready to Take a U-Turn?
Memory Verse: Hebrews 12:13

The past four days, you plowed through Scripture. Today it's time to apply what you've learned. You can have a head full of knowledge, but if you don't put it into practice, it fails to be life changing. When you are through with the questions, turn to the back of the book, where you'll find journal pages just for you to talk to God. Share what you've discovered so far.

If my parents didn't serve God, would I?

What would happen if the people I trusted the most (pastors, youth pastors, parents) failed or abandoned their beliefs? How would that affect my faith?

Apart from missions trips and outreaches, what would I tell people who questioned, perhaps even challenged, my beliefs and convictions?

Do my convictions come from a personal belief system? Can I back them up with Scripture? Have I taken time to ask more mature Christians to help me when I don't understand? Why or why not?

_____

_____

_____

How much does the following affect my faith? Rate yourself on a scale of 1 to 5—1 is "not really" and 5 is "oh yeah, that's me."

1. My Feelings: I go up and down depending upon whether I feel God or not. _____
2. My Traditions: My faith is all about weekly church attendance, youth group, or family commitment. _____

3. My Alone Time: I need music and hype to connect to God. _____
4. My Convictions: I've never taken the time to deepen my understanding of my belief system. _____

Talking with God

Lord, it's not always easy to lay it all out, but I'm exposing my heart and faith so that I can grow. Thank you for helping me to be honest with not only you, but myself.

2

Dependently Strong

[REAL QUOTE]
I have learned that prayer really works, which is something I always believed, but I had never really seen it because I had no faith. I have a challenge for all you whose life seems empty. Talk to God. Don't worry about saying the right things or how long you do it. Tell him what you feel. If you are mad at someone, tell God. If you are mad at God, tell God. And when you are done, ask God to help you. Just try it out.

—Austin E., age 18

My best friend was in trouble. She no longer took phone calls from her friends from church, not even from me. One night I waited for her outside her job. It was dark and I felt unsure as I waited under the dim streetlight. What would I say? Would it make a difference?

When Marcia walked out, I asked to talk. For the next hour, we sat in her car. She cried as she listed every reason she no longer wanted to be a Christian. She said that I was a reminder of a life she no longer wanted. Nothing I said made a difference.

I walked away with a heavy heart. I was confused because I didn't understand why she would give up a relationship with God. I didn't understand why our friendship couldn't continue even if she did. I could encourage her during the hard times. Maybe she would have someone to turn to when she started missing God.

But if I was honest, I wasn't just sad for her; I was worried about me. Who would be there with me when I needed that extra nudge? Who would I turn to when things went wrong at home?

The first time I went to youth service and she wasn't sitting beside me, I felt a little lost. As time went by, my friend's absence made me reach out to God even more. When things were difficult at school or at home, I talked to God about it just like I used to with her. I discovered that Jesus cared about the bumps and jolts in my life. He helped me through them. I still faced challenges, but I didn't feel alone.

Have you ever felt alone in your faith walk? If so, maybe you will understand how Matthew felt.

Matthew sat in his car and watched his best friend, Kris, walk across the parking lot. His dad had his hand on his shoulder, probably telling one of his famous stories. Kris's dad was a youth leader and most of the teens thought he was a cool guy. Kris's mom walked behind him with her two younger daughters. The girls were smiling and laughing at their dad.

Matthew frowned as envy put a move on his heart. He cared for Kris's family. They were like a second set of parents and he spent more time at their house than he did his own. Kris's dad helped out with special events at youth church and his mom signed up to be a sponsor for every trip.

Matthew thought about the scene he left that morning at his house. He was the only one up, as usual, on Sunday mornings. His dad had passed out on the couch after one too many drinks. His mom was out with her friends and came in late. His parents fought until two in the morning. Matthew shouted at them to stop and that brought the ugly scene into his room.

When the alarm sounded, Matthew was exhausted. He stumbled into the kitchen and rifled through the cabinets to find food, finally settling on dry cereal. He rinsed out a bowl because dirty dishes were stacked everywhere. He worked nights at the hardware store to pay his insurance and car payment, but tried to keep the place clean when he was not doing homework or at church. He had been busy lately and the chores had stacked up. His dad worked part-time and spent the rest of his hours drinking. Matthew's mom worked two jobs, so she was rarely home.

Things seemed easier when his dad was in prison. His mom was tired from working, but at least she seemed happy. Matthew kept the house up and worked to help pay bills. When Matthew's dad arrived home, the fights started all over again.

While his father was in prison, Matthew encountered God. One day Kris asked him to go to church. Matthew hadn't given much thought to religion, but that night he felt God for the first time. He loved the message that he heard and started going to church the next week. Soon he was attending whether Kris went with him or not. Matthew formed a tight relationship with the youth pastor and his wife. He even served on the leadership team. A lot of things turned around in his life, but he prayed every day for his parents to go to church with him. He wasn't looking for a perfect family. He just wanted his dad and mom to discover what he had.

Every time he brought up the subject his dad ranted about hypocrites, and then his mom got that tight look about her mouth that meant she wasn't comfortable with the conversation.

Matthew hated to admit it, but sometimes he almost hated Kris, especially when he griped about his parents being too involved. Kris wasn't trying to be a jerk; he just didn't know what he had. Matthew sat in the car for a few minutes longer. He asked God to remove the jealous thoughts. He gripped the steering wheel and prayed about his disappointments.

God's Spirit touches our spirits and confirms who we really are. We know who he is, and we know who we are: Father and children. (Rom. 8:16)

As he prayed, something huge occurred to him. Maybe Kris wasn't the only clueless one. Matthew's mom and dad might not be on board with his faith, but he wasn't alone. He had a heavenly Father who loved him more than anyone on earth.

HEART CHECK

You are strongest when you depend on God.

Having people support you in your faith is a gift, but God is ultimately your source. You can depend upon God to lead you.

Have you ever needed clear direction? I'm not talking about finding your way to the mall, but making choices and taking steps that are healthy and lead you in the right way.

What do you do if you feel God calling you to ministry, but you don't know what to do next? What do you do when your closest friends are going down a route that you know isn't for you? Who do you turn to when your girl breaks up with you and your heart feels broken?

You turn to God.

Let's talk about the mistakes people make when they need God the most.

Mistake 1: Pushing God Away When Times Are Tough

I was talking to a teen struggling with an eating disorder and with self-injury. She later wrote me an e-mail. It read:

I am on my own path. If I cut myself, it is because I choose to. If I lose five pounds and my parents worry about how much I've lost, it's not their battle. It is mine. I know that you love me, but you can only be in my life if I allow you in.

This beautiful girl chose a lonely path. In her thinking it is a strong road because she does not have to depend on anyone, but she fails to understand that healing and strength come when you allow God and godly people who care about you to walk with you through the hard times.

There's nothing wrong with being independent, but the more you leave God out of your decisions, the weaker you become. You can plunge ahead and carve out your own path, but when you ask God for direction he shows you roads you might not see on your own. He helps you with the tough stuff.

Jesus knows what it is like to feel betrayed and rejected. He understands pain and temptation. He sees the hard times, but also knows your future. When you call on him, he hears you.

When Matthew recognized his jealousy of Kris and his family, he could have hidden it but instead he invited God to help him through it. It didn't change Matthew's situation, but it did give him strength. It helped him to look beyond the circumstances and embrace the truth that God was his father.

> I know what I'm doing. I have it all planned out—plans to take care of you, not abandon you, plans to give you the future you hope for.
>
> When you call on me, when you come and pray to me, I'll listen.
>
> When you come looking for me, you'll find me.
>
> (Jer. 29:11–13)

Making It Real

When you exclude God from the tough times or situations, you're not hiding the problem. God knows how many hairs are on your head from day to day. He's aware of who you are and what you need. Why not allow the one who knows you best to join your day-to-day journey? He's got a life-map with your name on it.

Mistake 2: Not Giving God the First Opportunity

I had a friend who prayed over everything. She asked God to help her find a great pair of shoes and prayed when she lost an earring. When she pulled into a parking space, she stopped to praise God as if angels flew over her vehicle like a heavenly GPS. It seemed a bit extreme at times, but there is an opposite attitude, when God is nonexistent in your decisions until you hit Mount Hercules, a problem or situation so big that you know you can't handle it on your own. At this point, God becomes your spiritual "last straw." All the things that you normally trust have failed, so you rub the magic lamp and call on God.

That's not faith. That's desperation.

When Kris's best friend, Matthew, started coming to church, Kris was pumped. He and Matthew had been friends for more than three years, and Kris talked to him about all the fun stuff they did at church. One day Matthew said he would come and made a decision to follow God.

Then something weird happened.

It was like they were on the starting line and Matthew jump-started the race. He sprinted ahead of Kris spiritually in no time. Kris knew that Matthew's life wasn't easy, but he seemed to trust God no matter what. His faith was deep. Every time he looked at his friend, Kris felt like he had missed an important piece of the puzzle.

> Don't act thoughtlessly, but try to understand what God wants you to do. (Eph. 5:17 NLT)

One day Kris finally found the missing piece. Though his friend started later in the game, he turned to his faith for direction. It was a step that Kris had overlooked. He hadn't faced any large crises and didn't feel the need to ask God for direction. Why would you ask God for guidance when everything is running smooth?

One day Kris got alone with his buddy, and they had a long talk. Kris admitted he was swimming in the shallow end of the spiritual pool and wanted more. Matthew shared with him how God helped him, not only with the big stuff at home, but with decisions regarding his future, his relationships, and even things like jealousy.

Matthew and Kris made a pact to meet once a week as accountability partners so they could study the Bible and pray for direction. Within a short time, Kris was swimming in the deep end. He loved and appreciated his family and church, but was connecting with God in a whole new way.

Making It Real

Do you give God the first opportunity in your decisions? Not just the big stuff, but the everyday things like how to respond to a hurtful comment; what to do when you have to make a moral choice; who to date or when it's the right time. It's amazing how many of those seemingly minor choices become important if you make the wrong decision.

> If any of you lacks wisdom, he should ask God, who gives generously to all without finding fault, and it will be given to him. (James 1:5 NIV)

God will give you wisdom when you ask for it. Do you turn to God when you are offended, or do you hash it out with your friends? Do you ask for guidance when you and your dad aren't getting along, or do you let your emotions tell you how to respond? Who do you trust when you could easily cheat and take a higher grade but want to do what's honorable?

The more reliant you become on God in your choices, the stronger you become as a believer. When you learn to follow God in the big and small stuff, you follow in footsteps that are far bigger than your own. They take you in an entirely different direction than

**INTO ME
SEE**

Is God a
part of my
decision-
making
process?

your feelings, the advice of well-meaning friends, and the culture of this world.

Mistake 3: Leaving Your Road Map in the Glove Box

Have you been in the car with somebody who ignores the map in the glove box because she knows the way, even though you've been circling the same highway for over an hour? Doesn't that just seem . . . well, dumb?

It's the same with your spiritual life. The Bible is the ultimate road map. It covers every issue that could ever possibly come up.

Wait a minute! The Bible doesn't talk about masturbation, smoking, or drugs. It doesn't seem to address the topics that really matter to your life right now.

Let's take dating, for instance. The Bible doesn't say anything about dating because fathers arranged marriages for their sons and daughters in that culture. But, what about some of the issues related to dating? Here are just a few:

- How to treat others
- How to love another person
- Having deep relationships with nonbelievers
- Sexual purity

The Bible offers a road map to the heart issues on dating. If you desire to go out with (or date) a person who doesn't know God, you can investigate Scripture on the heart issues of this topic and discover that it's not part of God's plan. Second Corinthians 6:14 says, "Don't become partners with those who reject God. How can you make a partnership out of right and wrong? That's not partnership; that's war. Is light best friends with dark?"

Making It Real

What are your heart issues? Are you leaving God out of your choices? When you look for a solid foundation upon which you can build your convictions, you find a helper. The Bible is a light to help you find your way. With every decision, you have the help of the Holy Spirit.

> I'm no longer calling you servants because servants don't understand what their master is thinking and planning. No, I've named you friends because I've let you in on everything I've heard from the Father. (John 15:15)

The Bible is one road map to help you become dependently strong. Prayer is another. Prayer is an RSVP for friendship with God. I've never yet met a teen who lost their way while spending time with God every day. They found a very deep well where they could tap into healing, peace, guidance, and direction.

> But don't let it faze you. Stick with what you learned and believed, sure of the integrity of your teachers—why, you took in the sacred Scriptures with your mother's milk! There's nothing like the written Word of God for showing you the way to salvation through faith in Christ Jesus. (2 Tim. 3:14–15)

Another great road map is the people God places in your life. It's no accident that I'm listing them last. We often put people first and that can be confusing. If you talk to five people, chances are great you'll hear five different opinions. That's why you talk to God first and then check out what the Bible has to say about it before you talk to others.

That doesn't mean that people aren't an important part of your faith journey. Godly people—family, friends, and those in ministry—love you and normally have your best interest at heart. Surround yourself with friends who will be truthful, even when you don't want to hear it. Don't be afraid to ask people to pray for you.

Never underestimate how amazing it is to have a parent or grandparent who loves you and loves God. Though you may not always agree with their advice 100 percent, if they love God and their lives show it, you've been given something very special.

When you look to the Bible, prayer, and godly people for direction, you eliminate much confusion. It doesn't make the ride trouble-free, but it does give you clear direction. You know which way to turn, who to trust, and you never wander alone.

That's real strength!

Crucial Question: Do I Push God Away in the Tough Times?
Real Scripture: Luke 4:1–13

Jesus had just experienced the greatest moment of his ministry. Think about it! God parted the clouds and announced in a voice no one could mistake:

"Here's Jeeeeeeeeeeeesus! My one and only son."

Every person standing in the crowd had to admit that this was the Messiah, the king they had been waiting for their entire lives.

It was a great time to celebrate his newfound fame, but instead the Holy Spirit directed him out of town and into the wilderness where he fasted for forty days.

He was hungry and his body was tired when a visitor approached. It was the enemy, Satan, the spiritual darkness Jesus had come to battle. Satan circled like a lion stalking injured prey.

> The devil said to him, "If you are the Son of God, tell this stone to become bread." (Luke 4:3 NIV)

Making It Real

Satan landed a series of verbal kidney punches, tempting Jesus with food, material goods, and a promise of power. Though Jesus was and is the Son of God, he experienced everything that you and I do. He was isolated and hungry; he had slept in the open air and dust and among wild animals. He knew that rejection and death waited for him in his ministry. It was far less than what a king deserved.

Satan caught Jesus in a tough situation and tempted him. It went something like this:

Smack:	You're hungry. Turn the stone to bread.
Right back at you:	Man does not live by bread alone.
Smack:	Worship me and I'll give you all authority and splendor.
Try this one on for size:	I worship the Lord God and serve him only.
Smack:	Throw yourself from this high point and let angels catch you.
Catch this:	The Word says not to test God. Besides, I know whose I am.

Jesus countered every illegal move with scriptural truth. This counterattack not only forced Satan to leave, it brought light into a very dark place. Jesus was no longer alone in his battle.

When you hit a snag, what is your response? Do you invite God to join you or do you isolate yourself and let Satan push you around? God promises that he will never leave you. Take him up on that promise. He, and the Word, will keep you strong in the tough times.

_____

_____

_____

Talking with God

I will turn to you, God, search out truth about my situation in your Word, and ask others to pray for me when I'm weak. I become strong as I let your light shine in the dark places.

DEVO DAY 2

Crucial Question: Do I Give God the First Opportunity?
Real Scripture: 2 Samuel 11:1–27

Oh, what a tangled web we weave when first we practice to deceive!

David was trapped in a web of lies. It all started when he accidentally saw a beautiful woman taking a bath. He could have turned away, but he didn't. That choice led to another, and soon he was so deep in his own deception that he was drowning.

David didn't talk to God because he knew what he was doing was wrong. He just kept plunging deeper and deeper into the lies, and along the way, he ruined a few lives.

> After the time of mourning was over, David had her brought to his house, and she became his wife and bore him a son. But the thing David had done displeased the LORD. (2 Sam. 11:27 NIV)

David got the girl, but he lost much more than he gained. What if he had given God the first opportunity when he saw Bathsheba on the rooftop? It was a perfect time to ask God for help. Instead, he plowed on alone and took a path he never intended.

Making It Real

It's not that you aren't capable of making great choices on your own. You have a lot of tools to help you make decisions. One is common sense. Another is integrity. You have parents and friends. You even have books like this one!

But you also have God on your side. Giving him the first opportunity is important because it gives you discernment; that's the ability to know what is true and what is a lie. Discernment helps you walk away from spiritual traps.

When you feel doubt, talk to God. When you sense that something's just not right, slow it down and get alone with your Savior.

How many lives were impacted by David's lack of discernment? How would this story be different if God had been given first opportunity to help David with his temptation?

_____

_____

_____

Talking with God

God, I need discernment. Give me eyes to see and ears to hear what is false and what is true.

DEVO DAY 3
_____

*Crucial Question: Do I Ask God for Direction When the
Choice Isn't Clear?*
Real Scripture: Acts 9:1–9; 16:6–10

Paul was traveling to preach the good news to Gentiles. He had
his trip figured out until God threw a kink in his plans. The Holy
Spirit stopped him in his tracks and said, "Wrong way, dude."

This wasn't the first time Paul heard the voice of God. When he
was Saul instead of Paul and on a rampage to destroy Christians, a
blinding light served as a spiritual stoplight. He was blind for three
days and then his eyes were opened, both literally and spiritually.

Paul knew to pay attention when God spoke.

He could have launched a quick opinion poll, but he didn't. He
obeyed and turned in an entirely different direction. Taking one
road over another might seem like a small thing, but the Holy
Spirit saw something Paul didn't. There was danger ahead! But
that is only part of the story. There also were people in Macedonia
praying, people who were desperate for help. Paul's arrival would
be the answer to their prayers.

> During the night Paul had a vision of a man of Macedonia
> standing and begging him, "Come over to Macedonia and help
> us." (Acts 16:9 NIV)

Making It Real

God knew what was going on even when it was unclear to Paul.
How do you know that the choice you just made is the best choice?
What do you do when you've fallen for that godly guy or girl who
used to be just a friend? What about the issues that everyone
calls "gray"? Your mom says one thing. Your friends say another.

Everyone is doing it. The Bible says zilch. How can a person make the right decision when the answer isn't clear?

When your heart is slamming in your chest and you can't find peace, that's a red flag telling you to stop long enough to check in with God. It may be that God is directing you to a less-traveled path. Pray, listen, and obey. But if you are unsure, check out the heart issues. If your mom is saying no and you think nothing is wrong with what you want to do, the heart issue may be as simple as "honor your mom and dad."

What is your spiritual road map? Think about who or what you turn to first when you have an important decision to make. Share your thoughts.

_____

_____

_____

Talking with God

God, you know me better than anyone else. You know my motives. You even know what my future could be if I listen to and obey you. Thank you for your Holy Spirit, for Scripture, for godly friends and family, and for your direction.

DEVO DAY 4

Crucial Question: Do I Study the Bible for Myself?
Real Scripture: 1 Timothy 4:1–16

Your best friend calls and wants to meet you at the new skate park in a nearby city, but he forgets to tell you how to get there. You grab a phone book, close your eyes, and let it fall open. Then you stab the open page with your index finger.

Voilà! You open your eyes and read what you've found: Curl Up and Dye Beauty Salon, 68912 N. Hairline Avenue, 555–2389.

You're no closer to finding directions than when you first started. Many believers, even adults, use this same method to get direction from Scripture. It's not that God won't speak to you in creative ways, but there are practical methods that can help you study the Bible.

Making It Real

> Don't let anyone look down on you because you are young, but set an example for the believers in speech, in life, in love, in faith and in purity. (1 Tim. 4:12 NIV)

Let's say that you want to start a new ministry, but you feel inexperienced and overwhelmed. You find a Scripture you believe is relevant to your situation (1 Tim. 4:12) but want to know more. Where do you begin? You can start by asking the 5 *W*'s: who, what, why, where, and when. Let's try it now. Got your buzzer finger ready? Let's play WWWWW!

Who was the author of 1 Timothy?
Bzzz: Paul the apostle. He was Timothy's mentor and an experienced missionary. He traveled long distances to preach and help start new churches.

What is the book of 1 Timothy?

Bzzz: It's a personal letter from Paul to Timothy.

Why did Paul write this letter?

Bzzz: There were two reasons. The first was to encourage
         Timothy. The second was to give him practical tips to
         help him in ministry.

Where was Timothy?

Bzzz: He was in Ephesus. Timothy was a leader in the church
         and tangling with problems. One dilemma was a group of
         teachers who created confusion because they wanted the
         main focus to be on the law rather than grace.

When did this take place?

Bzzz: The date isn't certain, but we do know it was early in
         Timothy's ministry.

Now that you have uncovered the 5 *W*'s, read the Scripture one
more time. What advice was Paul giving to the young minister?
How would this advice help you?

_____

_____

_____

Talking with God

You inspired every word of the Bible, God. Speak to me through
the Bible. Open my heart and my mind as I become a student of
your Word.

DEVO DAY 5

Crucial Question: Where Do I Find My Strength?
Memory Verse: 1 Timothy 4:8

You are taking your faith a little deeper. You've learned to turn to God first. You've discovered that there are road maps to help keep you on track. You've also learned how to become a student of the Bible. When you are through with the questions below, kick back to the journal and write down the new things you are discovering about God, his Word, and about yourself.

How many sermons have you heard in your lifetime? Compare that to the times you are alone with God. Are you a bottle-fed Christian or do you feed yourself? What is one change you want to make?

Think about a specific time when you were struggling. Name, in order, who you turned to for help. Where did God fit in? Did you find Scripture to help you? Which godly person did you ask for help, advice, or prayer?

_____

_____

_____

What would you do different next time?

How much does the following describe me (give it a 1 to 5—1 is "Not really" and 5 is "Oh yeah, that's me"):

- I trust only myself when I'm having a hard time. _____
- I am honest with God when I am struggling. I tell him everything. _____
- I have mentors. _____
- I struggle to understand the Bible. It doesn't always make sense to me. _____

- I want to take my faith deeper so I will ask for help. _____
- I realize that I am stronger when I depend on God rather than myself. _____

Talking with God

You are not only my Savior, but Jesus, you are the Lord of my life. I need your advice and I want to trust you. I invite you in to my struggles, and I invite you to join me in the fun and awesome times. I want you to be a part of every aspect of my life.

Part 2

DECISION

What Do I Believe?

Hello

Sitting all alone,
In the darkness of my home.
Wondering about my life,
All that it's cracked up to be.

My life is not to be ruled,
By any laws and regulations.
But to be guided,
By your Holy Presence.

It's when I'm one with you,
That my worldly desires slip away.
I just want to grow in you,
Until I am part of you.

When the measure of my heartbeat,
Matches your heartbeat,
That I am so in tune with you,
That I'm in step with you.

Every step that I move,
Draws me closer to you.
With each passing of every day,
It becomes easier to say good-bye.

Good-bye to my old ways,
And hello to better days to come.
                    —Sarah Bright, age 23

3

You and God

[REAL QUOTE]

I found a kitten and it was cold and dying. I warmed it up and it survived. Last night I was laying on my bed with the little lucky kitten on my chest. I thought that what happened to the kitten is what happened to us. Jesus picked us up out of the coldness of sin and warmed us up to God's love.

—Callie S., age 14

The first three days of the fast were the hardest. I thought about food all day long. Do you realize how many scrumptious food commercials there are? Soon I was fasting not only groceries, but also TV. I couldn't watch another ad about hot fudge sundaes with whipped cream on top!

I was fasting for my friend. He was on a spiritual journey, but didn't believe in Jesus. He took medication to sleep and another pill to help him make it through the day. I had prayed for him for a long time, but his struggle grew only more intense. One day we were talking and I asked what he needed from God.

"I don't believe in prayer," he said.

"I can believe for both of us," I said. "Tell me what you need from God."

The answer was quick. "Peace."

"Then I'll pray for peace."

He sighed and turned away. "Suzie, it's been so long since I've felt peace. You can pray if you want, but nothing will happen. You're asking for the impossible."

I wish I could say that I am super spiritual and that fasting is easy, but it's not. I'm good for one meal, but around the second, I'm looking for a cheeseburger. But this was different. I felt called to fast. Every time I wanted to cave in and drive to the nearest drive-thru, the Holy Spirit tugged at my heart. I was reminded that my friend was in a serious spiritual battle. Fasting was one weapon I could use to fight for him.

A few days after I ended the fast, I ran into my friend. We sat outside and talked and he shared a story. Earlier that week he had a terrible day at work and left. On his way home he had an accident; he hit a pole and it damaged his car. He sat in the car angry and overwhelmed.

As my friend told the story, I counted backward. His accident happened on the day I ended the fast. I sighed.

My friend continued his story.

"Guess what happened then?" he asked.

"I don't know. Did your car catch on fire or something?"

My friend laughed. "No, something much weirder. A feeling came over me while I was sitting in the car. I had a bad day. My car was wrecked. I didn't have money to tow it, but in spite of all of that it happened. It made no sense at all."

I stared at him. "What happened? What are you talking about?"

My friend looked the other direction and I barely heard his reply. "It was peace," he said. He turned and looked at me. "Suzie, I had almost forgotten what it felt like. It was so cool. Everything around me was going wrong, but I felt so peaceful."

Inside of me I did the happy dance. I wanted to tell my friend about the fast, but it wasn't the right time. God answered his prayer. He was gently showing my friend that he was real and could be trusted no matter the circumstances.

That day God showed me something very powerful as well. It was not just my friend who was learning to trust God, it was me too. Fasting was God's way of asking me to believe that he loved my friend as much as I did. Have you ever wondered if God cares about you or the people that you love? Do you question whether God is relevant?

Gabbi asked all those questions and more.

Gabbi carried a notebook filled with poetry and random thoughts. She designed her own blog and subscribed to a hundred of her best online blogging friends. They posted deep discussions about faith and whether God really mattered in today's society. Religion was an issue for Gabbi because she went to church two or three times a week, not because she wanted to, but because her dad said she should. He sold real estate and most of his clients were church members. Church was their bread and butter. She had heard her dad say that a thousand times.

Church was fun, at least on Wednesday nights. Gabbi had friends there who felt like she did. They liked parts of church, but not others. She liked her friends, the music, the fun things they did on Friday nights as a group, but there were too many people at her church who acted one way there and then lived a whole different lifestyle at school.

Gabbi decided a long time ago that she wouldn't call herself a Christian until she was willing to live it.

The next summer she visited a friend who lived in another city. They went to a youth service that wasn't much different than Gabbi's church; the room was packed with teenagers and there was a band and fun games and a sermon. Gabbi knew only her friend and for the first time in a long time she couldn't sit in the crowd and dissect the lives of the people around her. Without the distractions, she focused in on the youth pastor's message.

"What do you believe?" he asked.

I believe that people are hypocrites, thought Gabbi.

"A lot of people carry the label of Christian, but they never take it to the next level. Maybe you know someone like that."

Yeah, like Abbi and Makayla and Todd. Gabbi mentally counted the people, bending a finger for each one.

"But what about you? Have you pursued a relationship with God on your own? Have you discovered how relevant God can be in your life? Have you stopped to ask the important questions about faith?"

Gabbi sat back in her seat. *No,* she thought.

"If the answer is no, then why not?"

I've been looking at everyone else. To my dad, church is business. To my friends, it's a place to hang out. To me? She shook her head. *What is God to me?*

That night Gabbi wrote in her blog:

> I talk a lot about God, mostly seeing him through other people. But I've focused so much on everybody else that I've never looked at myself. Who is God and what does that have to do with me? Does he know that I exist? Is there more to faith than sitting in a crowd of people who say they are Christian? I don't know if I'll ever find the answers, but I've decided to begin my search. I'm not sure what I'll find, but at least I will have asked the questions for myself.

Gabbi started her personal quest. She wasn't trying to change her life or live up to anyone's expectations. She just wanted to figure out things on her own. The answers she unearthed changed Gabbi, not overnight, but little by little. She was still writing poetry, still questioning, but God was making sense to her now. Faith became a whole lot bigger than selling real estate or hanging with friends.

It was personal.

Let's talk about a few of the questions Gabbi asked:

Relevant Question 1: Who Is God?

Is Jesus just another religious option? Is he a boomerang god, poised to spring from heaven and bonk you when you do wrong? Is he the guy in the picture with the white robe and blue sash carrying the lamb under his arm?

HEART CHECK

Don't be afraid to ask questions about God and your faith.

> In the beginning was the Word, and the Word was with God, and the Word was God. He was with God in the beginning. Through him all things were made; without him nothing was made that has been made. (John 1:1–3 NIV)

In the Bible, a guy named John was Jesus' best friend. He called Jesus the "Word." The Greek definition of *Word* is *logos,* which means "God desires to speak divinely to humans."

John introduces a Savior who wants to talk with every one of us. That busts the stereotype of a distant God sitting on a throne supervising heaven and earth, and it totally embraces the New Testament Jesus who walked, slept, and ate among his friends and hung out with those who didn't know anything about Christianity.

Jesus was full of life! And yet he was fully God. He performed miracles that changed families, healed the sick, and recovered the lost. He brought dead people back to life. He gave people a second chance when they no longer believed in themselves. In spite of all of that, some still didn't believe in him.

> He was in the world,
>   the world was there through him,
>   and yet the world didn't even notice.
> (John 1:10)

Why was that? Jesus wasn't what they were expecting. They were looking for a warrior, a hero to rescue them and build a kingdom. They wanted power and flash and dazzle, and failed to realize the power of love, healing, mercy, and grace.

Making It Real

A girl in my D-class (discipleship class) brought a Jesus character doll to class one Sunday morning. The action-figure Jesus wore a white robe and blue sash. It had piercing blue eyes and perfect brown hair and fit neatly in Carrie's purse. You could hold the doll in your hand and make it disappear or appear at will.

Our cultural viewpoint says that God is small. Sometimes even his own followers make him no more than an action-figure god. They whip him out when they are in trouble, but otherwise tuck him away. They carve out the pieces of Christianity they don't like and reduce God to fit their idea or society's. They choose aspects of his character like love and mercy, but ignore justice and holiness.

The Jesus that John spoke about in his gospel doesn't resemble an action-figure Jesus. John paints a different portrait of who Jesus was. He reveals a God who existed from the beginning of time. Jesus was instrumental in the creation of the universe. As a man he changed lives through the powerful encounter on the cross that busted heaven and hell wide open.

He's still changing lives today. Think about the people you know whose lives are completely turned around by an encounter with God. I'm one of them. Knowing Jesus turned my life inside out when I discovered that he was real and that I mattered to him. I didn't meet an action-figure God. I met a supreme Savior who, as big as he was, still wanted to know me on a personal level.

> But whoever did want him,
>   who believed he was who he claimed
>   and would do what he said,

He made to be their true selves,
their child-of-God selves.

(John 1:12)

The truth is that discovering who God is helps you find your true self. You get to see through the eyes of a God who knows you better than anyone else. The more that you learn about him, the more you understand what it means to have him living inside of you. That's life changing!

Relevant Question 2: Who Are You to God?

Do you know that God sees you differently than others see you? He cuts through the labels and the stereotypes to define you in ways you might struggle to grasp. In the Bible, a guy named Simon received a name change.

> Jesus came back, "God bless you, Simon, son of Jonah! You didn't get that answer out of books or from teachers. My Father in heaven, God himself, let you in on this secret of who I really am. And now I'm going to tell you who you are, really are. You are Peter, a rock. This is the rock on which I will put together my church, a church so expansive with energy that not even the gates of hell will be able to keep it out." (Matt. 16:17–18)

Some versions say Cephas and others Peter, but both names mean *rock*. It was almost funny that Jesus would choose that name for Simon because he wasn't rock solid; at times he almost went out of his way to prove that. Even after he became a follower of Christ, he ditched Jesus at a time he was needed the most. So why would Jesus call him the Rock?

It was because Jesus saw something that Peter and others didn't. He saw Peter as the man that he could be and that he would be as he followed Christ. Have you ever felt disrespected? Maybe at times you even disrespect yourself. That happens when you fail or don't live up to your or others' expectations. It can also happen when people—whether a parent or people at school—typecast you, pushing you into a mold of their making.

After a while you might feel like a screw-up or start to define yourself by the things people say about you.

But God sees you in a way you might not see yourself. Why? Because he knows you! He sees the talents he placed inside you. He knows exactly what can happen when ordinary people—even those who might mess up from time to time—place their lives in his hands.

God created you for a reason, with a purpose, and with ingredients placed inside of you that are unique to your personality, hopes, and dreams. You may be quirky, fun, have your own sense of fashion, or dance to a different tune than anyone else. Have you ever stopped to think that God made you that way?

INTO ME SEE
If I defined myself, what words would I use?

Now that you've painted a picture of who you are, let's check out what the Bible has to say. This is the psalmist singing to his maker:

> You know me inside and out,
>   you know every bone in my body;
> You know exactly how I was made, bit by bit,
>   how I was sculpted from nothing into something.
> Like an open book, you watched me grow from
> conception to birth;
>   all the stages of my life were spread out before you,
> The days of my life all prepared
>   before I'd even lived one day.
>
> (Ps. 139:15–16)

God knew you when you were just a tangle of cells and potential in your mother's womb. He knew you before you knew yourself. Kind of blows the mind, doesn't it? He knows your past.

He knows your future. He knows what's going on in your family. He knows the stuff you're working on in your heart and the things that seem huge. He knows the desire you have to run after him. Or the times you feel nothing, but want to feel everything.

Does this change the way you see yourself? Drop the labels. Scoot the stereotypes out the door. Now, take a minute and look fully in God's mirror. What do you see?

Making It Real

When Jesus stopped to ask Peter, Andrew, Philip, and the others to follow him, he didn't run a credit check. He didn't ask for references. He simply asked them to follow him. Maybe you're not a star. You might even sound like a frog when you sing, or you are too shy to get up in front of the group and speak. Maybe you *are* the star. In spite of what you are labeled, God sees you through a lens of possibility. Before tattoos were cool, God engraved you on the palms of his hands. That is a reminder of what you mean to him. He remembers you. He knows your name. You matter to God. He promises to never forget you. I don't know about you, but that makes me feel safe. You are secure in the hands of a mighty God.

> See, I have engraved you on the palms of my hands. (Isa. 49:16 NIV)

Relevant Question 3: Does God and My Faith Make Sense in My World?

This was Gabbi's main question. Once she grasped who God was and what she meant to him, she was still stuck with a culture that said God didn't fit. She started studying the stories from the Bible. God was pretty awesome. He ripped down from heaven to divide the Red Sea in two. He sent his Son to earth, using the stars to point to the newborn Savior. He talked to people through burning bushes and sent food down from heaven like a cosmic fast-food chain.

But the burning question was: Is God still around today? Is he relevant in this culture? Is he aware of heavy issues like sex, self-injury, STI's, homosexuality, divorce, addiction, just to name a few?

> Jesus Christ is the same yesterday and today and forever. (Heb. 13:8 NIV)

This is the answer that Gabbi discovered: God doesn't change.

He's definitely relevant and he's aware of the hurts all around us. People are changed every single day because of an encounter with Him. There is a lady in my church named Kim. She celebrates every Sunday morning during worship. She is full of joy. Some might be put off by her enthusiasm, but she can't help it. You see, a few years ago she was sitting in a prison cell addicted to meth. She had no future. She was alienated from her son. She was facing a long sentence in jail, but the bars of that prison were nothing in comparison to the chains of addiction and hopelessness.

A team from our jail ministry visited her and told her about Jesus. Five years later she is still free from addiction, free from prison, and free to be her child-of-God self. In fact, she's leading the prison ministry and is a part-time chaplain at the prison. Every Sunday, there are people sitting by her who have just come out of jail. They come because they want what they see in her.

Is God still around? Yeah, he's here. And he's still changing lives and bringing hope!

> God's Spirit is on me;
>   he's chosen me to preach the Message of good news
>   to the poor,
> Sent me to announce pardon to prisoners and
>   recovery of sight to the blind,
> To set the burdened and battered free.
>
>   (Luke 4:18)

Miracles happen every day. Many of them are seen in the lives of people who come across Jesus for the first time. There's a lasting mark left on their lives. It is just as significant and real as the parting of the Red Sea or the burning bush. God walks right into the life of a new believer and starts a brand new work.

Do you know someone who needs to hear that God is relevant to them? That he cares about their circumstances? Think of two friends who need to know Him. Write their names down and put the paper where you can see it every day and pray for a miracle in their lives. In fact, why don't you pray for them right now?

Decisions

Until Gabbi started asking questions, she was on the outside looking in. Her perception of faith was based on superficial things. God was a sermon. He was a name on a T-shirt. He was missions trips and drama tours and Sunday school classes.

When Gabbi decided to make faith personal, her life reflected intimacy with God. She was still funny and snarky, but she saw the teens in her youth group in a whole new light. Yeah, there were people who put on a show, but there were others who were still learning how to serve God. It wasn't up to her to judge others. It was time to get serious about her own journey.

HEART CHECK
God cannot be confined to a T-shirt.

Gabbi's old friends were intrigued. They knew that her faith was sincere. Several started their own search to find relevant faith.

What about you? Have you taken the time to get to know God as God? Do you focus on him instead of people? Over the next five days, you'll start the process of searching for your own faith. We'll talk about building your own altar as well as sharpen your image of God.

You may decide to make some decisions along the way. Don't be afraid to ask questions. God's not afraid of your doubts or the fact that you are taking a closer look at your faith.

Crucial Question: Have I Built My Own Altar?
Real Scripture: Genesis 12:1–7

Abram was minding his own business when God asked him to move cross-country. He promised Abram good things were ahead if he took a giant leap of faith.

Abram was comfy. He was connected to friends and family. He worshipped with his neighbors in the local temple. He was rich and respected. He was also seventy-five years old! Can you imagine your great-grandfather loading up his earthly stuff and trekking across the desert on a camel? But Abram was also a man of God, so he loaded up his household, his family, and a bunch of livestock, and started on the journey.

Every time Abram stopped to camp, he went rock hunting. He searched for stones before he watered the cattle, donkeys, or oxen.

Why? To build an altar.

Sacrifices were required by God as a part of their unique way of life. Sacrifices were made for many different reasons, for celebration of holidays and special events, for worship, and for forgiveness of sin. But Abram built the altar for a more personal reason: to remind himself that wherever he was, whatever he was doing, no matter how unfamiliar it all seemed, he was a child of God. The sacrifice was an open profession of his faith. By this one act of devotion, he put first things first in his life.

Making It Real

Building an altar out of rocks might seem like a strange idea because it's not how we worship God today. We don't offer sacrifices because Jesus came as the ultimate offering for sin. With his sacrifice, he brought us a new way of life, and the old law code that the Israelites lived by isn't necessary any more.

> As a priest, Christ made a single sacrifice for sins, and that was it! Then he sat down right beside God and waited for his enemies to cave in. It was a perfect sacrifice by a perfect person to perfect some very imperfect people. By that single offering, he did everything that needed to be done for everyone who takes part in the purifying process. (Heb. 10:12–14)

On my desk I keep a rock that I picked up out of my driveway. It's not anything special, but it is a reminder to build my altar every day, to hang out with God no matter where I am in life or what I am doing.

Do you hang out with God? Do you have an alone place where you block out all the pressures, stress, and noise of your life? Do you turn off the hype so you can get real with God?

Go out and find a rock—I'm not talking about a boulder, just a small stone. You can carry it in your pocket or put it in your car or in front of your computer. The location doesn't matter. But when you look at that rock, think about your altar. Write down what having an altar (not a place, but a heart attitude) means to you.

Talking with God

Dear Lord, please help me to put first things first in my life. Thank you for the sacrifice of your Son so that I can come freely to you. God, wherever I am, whatever I'm doing, I want you to be a part of it.

DEVO DAY 2

Crucial Question: Who Is God to Me?

Real Scripture: Luke 24:13–49

"Describe God," I said to my D-class.

"He's my best friend."

"He never gives up on you."

"He's a friend who doesn't get angry when you make a mistake."

"He's there, no matter what. Even when I abandon him, he doesn't leave me."

"Talk to me about his holiness and power," I said. "Tell me who God is, not just as your best friend, but as *God.*"

I was met by blank stares.

The descriptions of God were semi-accurate. He is your best friend. He is long-suffering and merciful. He does promise to be with you forever. But what if these descriptions were of human best friends? Let's see what that would look like.

"Mariah is someone who's always there for me even when I fail her. No matter what I do to hurt her or myself, she takes me back."

"I can always count on my buddy, Aaron. I might not talk to him for weeks, but when I'm ready to hang out, he's there waiting for me."

These comments say a lot about the faithful friend, but they also reveal a great deal about the speaker—the person who isn't such a great pal.

Making It Real

Who is God to you? Is he a warm and fuzzy pair of slippers that you can slip on and off? Is he a faithful God who, like a Golden

Retriever, sits patiently until you are ready to play? Sometimes God can be all around you and you miss his greatness.

> When he was at the table with them, he took bread, gave thanks, broke it and began to give it to them. Then their eyes were opened and they recognized him. (Luke 24:30–31 NIV)

When we begin to have a deeper relationship with Jesus, he shows us who he really is. He opens up our eyes to see him in a new way. Jesus is more than a buddy. He is a holy God who wants you to be holy too! What he did on the cross covers all your sin, and now when you mess up and stumble, he forgives you and helps you find your way.

Define who God is to you and the type of friend you are to him.

_____

_____

_____

Talking with God

On a clear night, go outside and look at the sky. Find a place where you can watch the stars. Study the width and span of the heavens. Look at the universe and then yourself in comparison. How big is God? Thank God for who he is and who he's made you to be. Be as specific as you can.

_____

_____

_____

DEVO DAY 3

Crucial Question: What Is My True Identity?
Real Scripture: Psalm 139

Rahab was a prostitute. David took care of sheep. Zacchaeus was a tax collector. None of these were in the running to win Who's Who in Church Leadership. Their resumes might not impress you, but God saw something special in each of these people.

When they grasped their true identity, they found purpose. Rahab is listed in the family tree of Christ. David was the most famous king in the Old Testament. Zacchaeus became a friend of Jesus.

What is your true identity? Is it what people say about you? Is it your talent? Is it your family or what you own or the type of car you drive? It's none of the above.

Making It Real

You are God's child. You are custom-created by a God who knows you better than anyone else. He has a plan for you.

> God affirms us, making us a sure thing in Christ, putting his
> Yes within us. By his Spirit he has stamped us with his eternal
> pledge—a sure beginning of what he is destined to complete.
> (2 Cor. 1:21–22)

Diamond makers etch a small identifying mark on each diamond. You can't see it with the naked eye. If the diamond is stolen, a jeweler places it under a special light, the mark is revealed, and the diamond is returned to the rightful owner.

Sometimes people lose their way from God because of sin. There's no feeling so large as being lost and believing that no one is looking for you. This is the good news: God made you, he mapped out your days with purpose and destiny, and when you are lost he looks for you and reclaims you as his own. You're marked, but in a good way! You are his. When you seek to know God as his child, you find him. When you want to go deeper in your faith, you can.

> "You will seek me and find me when you seek me with all your heart. I will be found by you," declares the LORD. (Jer. 29:13–14 NIV)

You don't have to ask God to make himself available. He gave you full access to him through the cross. What he needs is access to you as you grasp your true identity.

Read Psalm 139:15–16 and describe who you are to God.

_____

_____

_____

Talking with God

Father, I'm yours. I'm marked by you. You knew me before I knew myself. You know the potential inside of me. You know what makes me happy and what makes me sad. You know when I feel lost, and you reach for me. You do this because you know exactly whose I am.

DEVO DAY 4

Crucial Question: Is God Relevant in My World?
Real Scripture: 1 Corinthians 13

Check out the latest headlines from some teen magazines:

- "Who Do You Want to Make Out With?"
- "Satisfy Your Sweet Tooth with These Sweet Girls"
- "Hair, Cleavage, Teeth—Online Beauty Poll Shows Which Celebs Have the Goods"

Every day the media sends you zillions of messages about what matters in our culture. And according to these headlines, what matters are the external things: fashion, hair, and body. But here you are trying to live by a whole different set of values. The Bible tells you that God values you no matter what. So you are in a constant tug-of-war between what our culture thinks is important, and what the Bible tells you is important.

So where do you go for the real issues that you face? And does God really care about the questions and pressures of your everyday life?

Every day I receive e-mails from teens around the world through Real Teen Faith online. The biggest struggle that teens want to talk about is guy/girl relationships.

So let's talk about dating. Instead of the Elim-a-Date philosophy, the Bible offers what I call the *eliminate* philosophy. It helps you create standards. It teaches you how to choose wisely and also explains why you should eliminate some relationships before they ever begin. Though the Bible doesn't talk about dating, it gets right to the heart of how to have a healthy, long-lasting, committed relationship. This is just a sampling of what you might include on your *eliminate* list:

1. The person I choose will treat me with kindness and want the best for each of us (Matt. 22:37–40).
2. The person I choose will love God, not just go to church (Matt. 22:37–38).
3. The person I choose will be someone I can trust (1 Cor. 13:4).
4. The person I choose won't ask for what I cannot or should not give, but will find fun and cool things we can do together as we honor God (2 Tim. 2:22).
5. The person I choose will have hopes and goals and be strong in character.

> Love never gives up, never loses faith, is always hopeful, and endures through every circumstance. (1 Cor. 13:7 NLT)

The biblical message is that you are worth more than a five-minute hookup. You are worth more than what society tells you you're worth.

The truth is that God can really help you with your choices on dating, sex, and any other issue you might encounter. He has so much in his Word to help guide you through the maze of cultural messages. Invite him into your everyday world starting right now.

Talking with God

Father, don't let me forget my value in your eyes. I invite you to be a major part in all of my choices, especially with my relationships. Help my choices to honor you and your plans for me.

Crucial Question: How Do I Apply This to My Faith Life?
Memory Verse: Hebrews 6:1

This week you've discovered what it means to build your own altar. You've also explored three very important questions (share your answers):

1. Who is God?

_____

_____

2. Who am I to God?

_____

_____

3. What does faith have to do with my everyday life?

_____

_____

Have I ever made God small? How did that affect my faith? What shaped my view of God?

Do I reserve God for emergencies? How would my relationship with him change if I made him a part of my everyday choices?

_____

_____

_____

God knew me before I was born. He knows my future. If I look at myself through his eyes, how does that change my perception of myself?

Am I guided by cultural messages? Do I search Scripture and pray about issues of the day? Who or what do I normally allow to guide me in decisions and opinions?

_____

_____

_____

Now it's time to apply what you've learned about what you believe. Flip to the end of the book and share your thoughts in your journal.

Talking with God

Take a minute and create your own prayer. Share with God what you are learning and what you hope for at this time in your journey.

Dear God,

_____

_____

_____

_____

——————————————— **Part 3**

DILEMMA

Who Do I Trust?

When Plans Change

I had big plans for the summer of my junior year of high school. I planned a mission trip to Jamaica. I planned to work on the elite security team at Sonshine, a three-day music festival. I planned to get in shape for football. I planned on being a starter for my senior year as a football player. And with any leftover time I planned to work.

My plans didn't include being diagnosed with Osteasarcoma, bone cancer. My plans didn't include spending up to a week at a time in the hospital receiving chemo.

Personally, I thought my plans lined up with God, but I realized that God has great plans for us. I would much rather follow the plans of my Creator than my own plans. Jeremiah 29:11 talks about what God has planned for our lives. "'For I know the plans I have for you,' declares the LORD, 'plans to prosper you and not to harm you, plans to give you hope and a future'" (NIV).

Those are the plans I want to follow!

The plans that I had for the future never took place, but I've already seen examples of God's plans for my life. I know that God has much bigger, greater plans in store for me. I might not know them yet, but I trust that God does and that he's got his eye out for me.

He will never leave me nor forsake me. He is the master planner.

—Derek Hanisch, age 18

4

Trusting God

Each day of my life it's like I am waiting for something new.
Perhaps it's you, God.

—Elisabeth V., age 14

I was sitting in the front row praying for the teens in front of me.
I didn't know what their struggles were; I just prayed that they
would trust God. I had shared a simple message about giving God
everything so that you can find real treasure.

I watched fifteen-year-old Skyler. He normally slipped out to
hang out with friends before the altar call. But this night was different. When I was through speaking he gave me a huge hug. "I
want to find that treasure," he said. He found a quiet place where
he could pray alone.

Every teenager in the room had a different story. Some had
families that attended church with them, while others came alone.
Some were leaders in the youth group, while others were involved
in different ways. There were all sizes, shapes, races, economic
backgrounds, and diverse circumstances represented that night,

yet most of them were searching for the same thing. They wanted to trust God, with their messes and mistakes, with their questions, with their problems.

For many of these teens in front of me, trusting God was an intricate issue. How do you trust someone so big and so distant? What if you fail in your faith walk? What if you are doing everything right and things still fall apart?

I remember my own struggles. God had taught me how to trust, but what word picture could I paint to show how to trust God in good and bad times?

As I thought about that, my attention was drawn away by the sound of crying. The youth pastor's eleven-month-old son was tired and cranky. He threw himself on the floor, arching his back, and wailing. The youth pastor was a tall, strong guy, kind of like Superman minus the cape. He reached down and picked up his son and cradled him in his arms. His little boy wrestled for a few moments, but his daddy held him close and whispered to him. Within minutes the child settled down and fell asleep, safe in his daddy's embrace.

It was as if God had given me a glimpse of himself. He is a father who is strong, yet gentle. He is firm, but loving. He reaches for his children when they are tired or restless and even when they are in rebellion and don't know where to turn. He guides them to a safe place.

God can be trusted! The dilemma is learning how to trust him and turn to him wherever you are and whatever you are facing. It seems easy to trust God when things are smooth, but it's a lot harder when you're coasting through life and you hit a brick wall that you didn't see coming.

That's what happened to Tate.

Tate pumped his arms and stared at the finish line. He punished every muscle, commanding his body to respond. He passed one runner, then another. Soon it seemed almost effortless. He crossed the finish line and threw his arms up in the air and the crowd cheered with him. His coach shouted out the time. Tate jumped in the air and pumped his fist. He had broken the state record in the 800 meter.

A month later Tate was on his way home from a church party. He called his dad to let him know he might be a few minutes late. As the phone rang, he thought about the party. The night was awesome. Calissa and he had talked seriously for the first time. She was not only beautiful, but she genuinely loved God. Things couldn't be any better. First the possibility of a state championship, and now this.

Life was sweet!

Tate thumped his knuckle on the steering wheel, smiling to himself as he waited for his dad to pick up.

"Tate?"

Just as he heard his dad's voice, a bright light blinded him and Tate threw a hand up over his eyes. The cell phone clunked on the floorboard and Tate sucked in his breath as the seatbelt pinned him to the seat. Glass shards hit his face like gravel. The air bag popped and then something like a 300-pound linebacker crunched into his lower body.

Tate woke up hours later in a sterile emergency room. His mom was crying. His dad stood nearby with his head bowed. The youth pastor and pastor consoled his mom. Calissa and several of his friends stood in a huddle by the door.

"Mom? Dad?" his voice croaked.

His parents walked quickly to his side.

That night Tate learned that a drunk driver crossed two lanes of traffic at 70 miles an hour and hit his car head on. Tate's dad had heard his son scream and he called 911, grabbed his coat and keys, and rushed out the door to find him. He found a swirl of blue and red lights flashing on the gruesome scene. Tate was trapped under the engine pushed through the dash. The drunk driver was dead.

When he arrived at the emergency room X-rays showed Tate's

hip, legs, and pelvis were broken. His body and face were bruised and peppered with glass cuts.

From that night forward, Tate's life changed. The hospital became home for two months. Tate had two surgeries and physical therapy. Calissa, Tate's buddies, and youth pastor came to the hospital almost every night to keep him company. At night Tate dreamed about running. He jerked awake in pain as his legs pushed against the 45-pound traction.

He left the hospital in a wheelchair. It took several more months to progress to a cane and then crutches. Tate worked hard. After eight months he was running again. He was in agony after every workout, but he pushed the pain aside with hard work, determination, and prayer that he would again be the athlete he once was.

After a year, Tate tried out for the track team. He wasn't fast or fluid like he was before the wreck, but he worked on his moves. He ran sprints. He ran up and down the stadium stairs until his track uniform was drenched in sweat.

At the first meet Tate lined up at the starting line. It felt good to be on the track with other competitors. Several slapped him on the back, congratulating him. The starter gun fired and Tate pushed off. He passed one runner, and then another. His hip ached. His legs screamed with pain, but it felt good. He wasn't running as smooth as he once did, but at least he was running. He had all season to work on his speed.

Tate felt a pop and grimaced in agony. He limped down the track, trying to shake it off. His kneecap twisted and Tate plummeted to the ground.

He could see his mom and dad's stricken faces as they leaned against the rails. He saw looks of sympathy on his teammates' faces. Everyone on the blue and white side stood to their feet, but Tate didn't want their sympathy. All he wanted was to be in the game. The pain in his knee was blowing him away, but it was nothing compared to seeing his dreams disappear one more time.

Tate started another journey just as difficult as the first as he

released his dreams. The doctor said ath-
letics were physically impossible.

You can
trust God
even when
life doesn't
make sense.

When he let go, he took the hand of God
and talked to him about his confusion.
When he was angry—which was often—
he was honest about it, but he took it to a
safe place of prayer where he could talk to
God. Tate learned a lot during that difficult
time. He thought he trusted God before, but it was easy because
things were going his way.

The true test came when he hit the hard times.

Let's talk about the times that it's not so easy to have confidence in God.

Dilemma 1: It's Hard to Trust When Life Isn't Fair

If you're breathing, you've figured that out that life doesn't always go your way. There was nothing right about a drunk driver
getting behind the wheel of a car and hitting Tate. It wasn't fair
that he worked so hard to overcome his injuries, only to get side-
lined in his first meet by a knee injury.

Tate's dreams were impacted by someone else's decision. At
times he was more than a little mad at God. Being an athlete
wasn't just playing the game; it was part of his identity and it was
his passion.

Where was God? Was he out patrolling the cosmos and too
busy dealing with other things?

> What's the price of a pet canary? Some loose change, right? And
> God cares what happens to it even more than you do. He pays
> even greater attention to you, down to the last detail—even
> numbering the hairs on your head! (Matt. 10:29–30)

Nothing happens when God isn't looking, because God is always looking. It's hard to understand how he can always see

anything and everything, but he does. And you know what? He actually cares about it.

In Bible times, songbirds like canaries and sparrows were the cheapest birds sold in the market. They were food for the poor. Yet as insignificant as sparrows or canaries were, God saw them. He watched over them. There is nothing in the whole of God's creation that he doesn't watch over and care about.

You can only imagine how much attention he pays to you!

Though the wreck wasn't fair, God was on the scene. His plans for Tate didn't go up in smoke because of the wreck or Tate's injuries.

There was a guy in the Bible named Job. He had a great family and was a wealthy and respected man. One day Satan asked if he could tempt Job.

INTO ME SEE

Do I realize that God is with me in the hard times, as well as the good?

"He's my faithful servant," God replied.

"That's why it's so easy to trust you," Satan said. "It's not hard to be faithful when things are good."

They debated back and forth and finally God relented. Though the Bible doesn't say why God allowed this, it does reveal that God trusted his main man, Job. Satan robbed Job of his wealth and his children. He swept away his home. He assaulted his health and plagued him with boils all over his skin. All that Job had left was a wife who nagged him and some friends who said all the wrong things. This isn't a pretty picture and it's a story that is easier to leave out, except sometimes life isn't fair and we need to be honest about that.

Why did a godly man endure so much? Job asked this very question.

> If only my anguish could be weighed
>   and all my misery be placed on the scales!
> It would surely outweigh the sand of the seas.
>   (Job 6:2–3 NIV)

Making It Real

Your dilemma may be the result of someone else's poor choice. It could be the messy aftermath of an accident. It might be that you were in the wrong place at the right time, or it might be a test to develop your character. Regardless of the situation, God hasn't abandoned you. His plan for your life continues. He's still your friend.

But do you know what every challenge has in common? Each one offers you an opportunity to trust God in a way you've never trusted him before.

Tate learned that he could trust God no matter what life handed him. At some point you will be affected by someone else's choice. But that doesn't mean that all your choices have been taken away. In fact, it's the beginning of many options. Tate could curse his life or hate the drunk driver. He could resign himself to a life without dreams, or trust that God still was in control.

> Then Job replied to the LORD: "I know that you can do anything, and no one can stop you." (Job 42:1–2 NLT)

Unfair situations happen, but they do not ruin God's plans.

When you trust God during hard times, you add qualities to your character such as compassion and patience. You grow spiritually as you learn to lean on something bigger than yourself and your circumstances. That knowledge will help you for the rest of your life, and it's something that no one will be able to take from you.

Dilemma 2: It's Hard to Trust When Things Change

We were traveling to Canada when I heard a thump, thump at the rear of our new truck. We were in Minnesota on a main highway so we exited toward Duluth. We drove around the curve of the highway and right in front of me was one of the most beautiful lakes I had ever seen: Lake Superior.

The sun sparkled on the surface. A bridge spanned the entire lake from one city to another. Fishing boats hugged the coast as fishermen searched for fish. We stopped at a tire store and bought a new tire, then detoured across the bridge. I rolled down my window and stared out as we traveled high above the water. I pointed out the fishing and sailing boats.

I didn't want to buy a new tire. It wasn't in our plans or our budget. The flat tire delayed our schedule.

But then there was Lake Superior!

God takes the detours and messes of life and shows us something beautiful.

> Don't you see, you planned evil against me but God used those same plans for my good, as you see all around you right now—life for many people. (Gen. 50:20)

Making It Real

Have you ever had things mapped out, only to experience change overnight? Your dad gets a promotion and you have to move to another state. Your parents decide to be foster parents and a new person disrupts the flow of family life. Grandma moves in and takes your bedroom. The girl you've dated for a year decides that it's time to take a break and then you see her on the arm of a loser.

Times like that jar the comfortable rhythm of your existence.

Tate could no longer play sports, but that didn't remove his passion. When he went to college, he took a journalism class. One assignment was to cover a local basketball tournament. Tate discovered that night that he loved writing about sports. It was different than running and feeling the wind at your back, but it was just as awesome, especially when his first byline hit the front page of the sports section.

Did the wreck change his plans? Yes, but Tate learned that dreams are like a river. If one channel closes, another can spring up. It wasn't God's desire that a drunk driver lose his life and impact Tate's dreams, but God was there with a big highway sign to help Tate in the crossroads. God showed Tate a different path that was just as relevant.

Sometimes the change is not the result of people or mistakes, but a definite chess move from God on your behalf. What if the move that you are resisting is a part of God's strategy? What if this unexpected move puts you in the path of someone you've never met before who needs to know you, whom you can impact? What if there is a new avenue or experience, one that you might not have tried before, that will prepare you for the future, and if God didn't intervene in his very "God-like" way you'd never go down that path? Your reflex reaction to the unexpected might be to think God wanted to disrupt your comfy world. But God always has something up his sleeve that you might not understand in the moment.

Don't limit God to operating within your comfort zone. As a follower of Christ you will continually be nudged, challenged, and stretched. Rather than asking "Why me?" would you consider asking, "What do you have for me now, God? What cool, amazing thing do you have up your sleeve?

Dilemma 3: It's Hard to Trust God When You Don't Know Where to Turn

Remember Job? Three of his friends, Eliphaz, Bildad, and Zophar, had tons of advice. They took turns debating whether he had sinned or if he was suffering because of a lack of faith in God. Job's wife even told him to curse God and die.

Great advice, right?

Wrong!

> Who is this that darkens my counsel
> with words without knowledge?
> Brace yourself like a man;
> I will question you,
> and you shall answer me.
>
> (Job 38:2–3 NIV)

Job pelted the heavens with honest questions: What's up with this, God? Where are you? Do you hear me?

God came back Jeopardy style and buzzed in with a few questions of his own.

Can you hold back the movement of the stars? Are you able to restrain the Pleiades or Orion? Can you shout to the clouds and make them rain? Can you make lightning appear and cause it to strike as you direct it? He reminded Job that he was bigger than circumstances and had his hand over Job's life—no matter if things were peachy or downright messed up.

Job buzzed back and won the million-dollar category of "Who is God?"

> Listen, please, and let me speak;
> You said, "I will question you, and you shall answer Me."
>
> I have heard of You by the hearing of the ear,
> But now my eye sees You.
>
> (Job 42:4–5 NJKV)

Some people call these moments epiphanies. They are light bulb moments. Flash, pop, the smoke clears, and suddenly everything makes sense. No matter how serious the situation appeared, God was with Job. God hadn't abandoned him.

After time, Job was given twice as much as before, but his riches didn't come from the 14,000 sheep or 6,000 camels or the 1,000 female donkeys. Job was wealthy in a way that had nothing to do with bling-bling. He received a glimpse of a sovereign God and learned what it meant to trust him when nothing else made sense.

Making It Real

Think about this. God isn't supposed to be reserved just for the tough stuff. You learn how to trust God when you partner with him on a daily basis, even in the smallest details.

Trusting God is like building muscle mass. You don't pick up 400 pounds on your first attempt. The first time you bench press, you might only be able to handle 40 pounds (okay, I can't even do that!). But every time you flex your muscles, you get stronger. God becomes your bench press. He's able to lift 4,000 pounds with a finger. He can help you lift far more than you can on your own.

You bench press when you give him first chance in every area of your life. You bench press when you pray over your relationships. You make your spiritual muscles work when you talk to God when you're angry with your parents. You work out when you ask him for help when you're studying for a Chem II quiz.

God is not limited to quickie prayers over pizza. And he's not on hold to show up like a superhero when the massive boulder life just placed in your path won't move.

When you trust God in the small things, it becomes instinct to turn to God—no matter how big or small the situation.

There are several key questions to help you take the issue of trust to the next level. Over the next five days, we'll explore those and you'll inch your trust factor to a brand new height.

HEART CHECK

God is not reserved as a backup for the big stuff or when others let you down.

Crucial Question: Do I Trust God When Life Is Unfair?
Real Scripture: Genesis 37:1–36

Eleven brothers stood in a huddle and watched their annoying little brother cross the field. While they waited, they plotted Joseph's death. It sounds like a bad reality television show, but it wasn't staged. Their father's favoritism made them angry. It didn't help when Joseph told them dreams of how they would bow down to him one day.

> "Let's kill him and throw him into one of these old cisterns; we can say that a vicious animal ate him up. We'll see what his dreams amount to."
>
> Reuben heard the brothers talking and intervened to save him, "We're not going to kill him." (Gen. 37:20–21)

Reuben convinced his brothers not to kill Joseph, but to throw him in a pit instead. Some Ishmaelites wandered by and Joseph's life completely changed when his brothers sold him as a slave. As Joseph was carted off on the back of a camel, he probably had some serious questions for God. The dreams hadn't said anything about slavery!

Making It Real

When God places a dream in your heart, it might be huge. Maybe it's serving as a missionary or a doctor or speaking the truth as a preacher. Maybe it's breaking away from your past and being all that God knows you can be. But what if the road to your wildest dreams becomes windy, bumpy, and scary? What if you hit a few detours, ones that take you through some pretty crazy terrain? The journey might get so long and confusing that you don't think you can make it. What if financial and practical problems stand between you and your dream? What if you're backhanded with a slice of life you didn't ask for and you don't know which way to turn? The question is not how big is the obstacle. It's, how big is God?

It wasn't just Joseph's brothers who were unfair to him. Later in the story his boss's wife accused him unjustly and he went to jail. While he was in jail he did a guy a favor and interpreted a dream. That guy said he would help him, but forgot.

Unfair! Unfair! Unfair!

None of that detoured God's dreams for Joseph. In the end, the man standing in front of his brothers was no longer a boy bragging about his dreams. He was strong and courageous. He had learned to trust God, even in the hard parts.

> Joseph was running the country; he was the one who gave out rations to all the people. When Joseph's brothers arrived, they treated him with honor, bowing to him. (Gen. 42:6)

Do unfair situations change God's plans? Why or why not?

_____

_____

_____

Talking with God

Jesus, I realize that you see so much more than I do. You know my future. You know the beginning, middle, and ending. Help me to trust you when life is unfair and continue to trust in your plan for me.

DEVO DAY 2

Crucial Question: Will God Show Me What to Do?
Real Scripture: James 1

If a soccer ref sees a player on the field about to make an illegal move, she throws out a yellow flag. The flag warns the player to think about the way he is playing. It gives the player a moment to think about the move he was making.

Caution!

Sometimes the ref throws out a red flag.

Foul!

This stops the play completely. The player might even have to sit on the bench or receive a penalty. The ref isn't just concerned with one player or one team, but the whole game. The yellow and red flags allow the game to be played with the best possible outcome for everyone on both teams.

Sometimes you receive a yellow flag. It's the Holy Spirit nudging you to slow down long enough to listen to the coach. When we pray and ask God to show us where to go, we might receive a green light or he just might throw out a red flag. If you sense that God is saying no, don't ignore it. Respect it. Learning to hear God is key to taking the right path.

How do you know if what you are hearing is God? What if it's just the hot dogs and chili you ate the night before? If what you are hearing contradicts the Bible, it's not God. It's as simple as that. He can't and won't go against his own word. When a teen says that God is telling her it's okay to date a guy who isn't a believer, then I crack open the Bible. She has misunderstood God's will for her because the Bible clearly says that missionary dating isn't in God's plan.

After you consult the Bible, the second step is to obey. Just because it's big or difficult doesn't mean that it's not spiritual. This is the same God who told Noah to build an ark, Gideon to go to war with only three hundred men, and Joshua to march around the walls of Jericho until they crumbled. When he straps you into the ride of destiny, he's the lead driver. He'll be with you even when it seems impossible.

But what about the signals that aren't so clear?

> If you don't know what you're doing, pray to the Father. He loves to help. You'll get his help, and won't be condescended to when you ask for it. Ask boldly, believingly, without a second thought. People who "worry their prayers" are like wind-whipped waves. (James 1:5–6)

When you do hear from God, act on it. Many times God shapes the events of your life so that it is clear which direction to take. When God puts someone who doesn't believe right in your path, you don't have to ask God if it's okay to tell him about Jesus.

When God talks to you, you feel peace, but you may still struggle with fear. Every time I speak in front of a crowd, I wonder if God knows what he is doing. But I have learned that if he asks me to do something, he'll be with me as I take that big step.

Making It Real

Have you encountered a situation where you felt God throw out a caution flag? Share that situation and how it turned out.

_____

_____

_____

Do you pay attention to the yellow and red flags God throws out on the field? Why or why not?

_____

_____

_____

Talking with God

God, teach me to listen to your voice. Let your Word be my guide. Teach me to wait when things are all murky and gray. Clear the muddy waters and show me the way.

DEVO DAY 3

Crucial Question: What if My Life Is Affected by Someone Else's Decision?
Real Scripture: Romans 8:26–39

Parker's dad was in the ministry. One day he left the church and his family for another woman. Overnight Parker's life changed from a PK to the guy everybody in town was talking about. He couldn't go to a high school football game without seeing people whisper. Worse, some people found him and gave long speeches about how sorry they were. He felt trapped, knowing that they were sincere, but hating the attention and words that made the pain only more intense.

Everything that Parker believed was tossed out by his dad's decision. It was his dad who prayed with him. It was his dad's sermons and advice that taught him how to be a Christian. When his dad decided to have sex with someone other than Parker's mom, nothing made sense anymore.

His mom was forced to find a job. Parker and his brother started mowing lawns to help with expenses. It was hard, but nothing was more difficult than walking into the church the first week after his dad left. He didn't realize how much his identity was wrapped around his old life. He felt lost.

They all did.

Making It Real

Parker's dad left chaos behind him and God grieved over that decision. How do we know that? In the Old Testament God grieved every time his children disobeyed and allowed sin to harm themselves and their families. It wasn't God's plan for Parker's father to lose his way.

Sometimes life slam-dunks you before you even had a chance

to get in the game and play some "D." That happens when your parents divorce or are fighting. It happens when your friend moves away and you feel alone, or when your boyfriend breaks up with you to go out with someone you thought was your best friend. Where do you turn in times like this? Perhaps by now I sound like a broken record, but God is your shelter during times like that. He's your safe place.

> What, then, shall we say in response to this? If God is for us, who can be against us? (Rom. 8:31 NIV)

You see, even when the people you love fail you, God won't. His love is bigger and deeper and wider than human love.

> No, in all these things we are more than conquerors through him who loved us. For I am convinced that neither death nor life, neither angels nor demons, neither the present nor the future, nor any powers, neither height nor depth, nor anything else in all creation, will be able to separate us from the love of God that is in Christ Jesus our Lord. (Rom. 8:37–39 NIV)

If people or their choices have hurt you, I'm so sorry, but may I make you a promise? God won't leave you or fail you. He won't turn his back on you. His love for you can't and won't be taken away.

Read Romans 8:37–39. Place your name in the Scripture. Make it personal. Share your thoughts about this promise.

_____

_____

_____

Talking with God

Dear God, sometimes I just need to find a safe place in you. It's risky for me to trust you because people have let me down, but, God, your love is different. You promise that you are with me always. Your love is greater than I can imagine and I open my heart to receive that love today.

DEVO DAY 4

Crucial Question: What if I Can't Trust Myself?
Real Scripture: Romans 7

Blake started messing around with pornography on the Internet. He soon discovered that it was an addiction stronger than any drug. Marissa loved a guy, but he was demanding too much from her. She finally gave in and now she's pregnant. The guy is nowhere in sight. What do you do when you fall? Do you lose everything that God has done in your life? Do you run away?

Jake did.

One day he was standing in the altars in love with Jesus, and the next night he was acting like a fool. One drink, his friend said. No big deal, right? One drink led to two and then more, and that led to choices he never would have made otherwise. The word got out. Jake knew what people were saying. It wasn't much different from what he was saying about himself. In his heart he still wanted God more than anything, but how could God trust him if he couldn't trust himself? Rather than talk to God about it, Jake ran away from his faith, his friends, his calling. Friends tried to reach out to him, but he shut them out. He let it drive him down a road of drugs and more pain.

One night Jake was alone. He missed God so much he couldn't stand it. He knelt on the floor of his room and asked God to forgive him. He wasn't sure what to expect, but was floored by the love of God that covered him like a blanket. Today Jake is in love with a beautiful Christian girl and studying to be in the ministry. His past is not pretty and there's no going back to change that, but he can go forward. He let God heal the past and give him back what he lost.

> It happens so regularly that it's predictable. The moment I decide to do good, sin is there to trip me up. I truly delight

in God's commands, but it's pretty obvious that not all of me joins in that delight. Parts of me covertly rebel, and just when I least expect it, they take charge.

I've tried everything and nothing helps. I'm at the end of my rope. Is there no one who can do anything for me? Isn't that the real question?

The answer, thank God, is that Jesus Christ can and does. He acted to set things right in this life of contradictions where I want to serve God with all my heart and mind, but am pulled by the influence of sin to do something totally different. (Rom. 7:21–25)

Making It Real

Paul wanted God, but his flesh reached with greedy fingers for sin. What's a believer to do?

Reach:	Jesus Christ fights the enemy for you. Ask him to help when temptation calls your name.
Repent:	Apologize and ask God to forgive you when you sin.
Receive:	Accept the true grace of God.
Restore:	Let God put you back on track.
Remember:	Learn from your mistakes. Stay away from traps that trip you up.

Sin grieves God and there are consequences, but you've not lost God's love. You're not kicked out of the heavenly program when you fall. These are your choices: stay down or get up. Every believer struggles with temptation and sin. It's the age-old battle of the flesh versus the spirit, but you are not defenseless. You can trust God to help you mature spiritually and to cover your sins with the power of the cross. What if it's huge? Then you deal with the consequences and learn from them, but get up! Don't let your failure define your life. Start fresh with God's help.

Have you ever let sin rob you? Think about the five *R*'s. Apply them to your situation.

Reach_____

Repent_____

Receive_____

Restore_____

Remember_____

Talking with God

Lord, you know my battles. You know the war that rages inside of me at times. Teach me how to recognize the traps that rob me of what I love—your presence, your call, your destiny. Thank you that I am not alone in my battle and that I can turn to you.

DEVO DAY 5

Crucial Question: Am I Ready to Trust?
Memory Verse: Romans 11:22

Faith. Belief. Hope. Conviction. Confidence. Assurance. Expecta-
tion. Anticipation. These are strong words. Like a seed rising from
the soil, these characteristics grow when you trust God.

Are you ready to plant seeds of trust? It's vital that you take
this step because a lack of trust is at the heart of most dilemmas.
Rather than being stuck in a situation you can't get out of, you can
discover beforehand how amazing it is to trust God. Let's explore
this more.

What is one logical step you can take when you feel doubt?

_____

_____

_____

Your destiny is like a map. Think about where you are right
now. What is God showing you?

_____

_____

_____

Do you limit God to operate within your comfort zone? Name
one way God can help you in this area. Don't be afraid to ask God
for his help.

_____

_____

_____

Are you willing to sacrifice feelings, time, relationships, to obey God?

_____

_____

_____

Go to the back of the book and journal your thoughts about this chapter. Write a poem, song, or quote that describes what you are learning about trusting God.

Talking with God

Dear Jesus, you trusted God's plan even when people failed you. You loved and lived life to the fullest. Help me to live life like that. Help me to reach for you no matter where I am or what I am going through.

——————————— Part 4

DESTINY

What Does God Want from Me?

My Commission

An empty canvas stands
 before me
Yet to be displayed.
My commission was
 commanded clear,
Yet what will be portrayed?

As I raise the tainted brush
And lay my strokes of red,
Some splattered and
 splotched, some fluent and
 fragile;
What is compiled instead?

Seeping through each line I
 lay
Pieces of my life I lend.
Some harsh and hurtful, some
 fond and cherished,
Though what shall be my
 end?

As light wanes from kindled
 flames,
My sight is slowly lost.
Arm and brush ache to rest,
But what shall be the cost?

For should stroke cease as
 fingers tire,

My assignment left to lie.
Though I could idle to endless
 hours,
Why then did he die?

Life was paid to purchase this
 piece
And all was sincerely given
So that I could grasp my goal;
 my life.
This is why I'm seriously
 driven.

So on I paint though sight
 should dim;
Though bones grow crooked
 and bent.
Still never losing dream nor
 drive
Reflecting on resources spent.

For trickling from his dying
 veins
My red paint and my mission
To create beauty from his
 death;
This is my commission.
—Rachael L. Joseph, age 15

5

Drop Your Nets and Follow Me

Our culture demands that we all be the same. Everyone is always rushing and running to look like everyone else. Although many people strive to keep their individuality they often fail. By striving to be different they lose who they really are and in turn become another casualty. Unless we stop striving to be someone we are not, we will all lose our generation to the one thing we think we got rid of: conformity.

—Brian P., age 16

The stars seemed a million miles away, sparkling like tiny diamonds in the sky. Water lapped against the side of the rough-hewn canoe. There were four of us perched in a row. As my eyes became accustomed to the dark I saw outlines of trees along the shore.

"We'll stay away from the trees," the guide said. He pointed to the treetops. "Anacondas," he whispered.

Anacondas. Crocodiles. Piranha.

I was so far out of my league it was ridiculous. We were living on the Amazon in the rain forest of Brazil for a week to help with a medical clinic. I volunteered to help. I worked in the eye clinic all day and sat on the boat at night, swatting away the mosquitoes that swarmed. When one of the guides asked if anyone wanted to crocodile hunt, I threw up my hand and said yes.

I thought he was joking.

Three guys from the construction team climbed in the canoe with us. As the large boat faded in the distance and darkness covered us, one asked cheerfully, "So, what are we really doing?"

The guide put his finger to his mouth. He handed the first man in the canoe a flashlight and asked him to shine it over the water. Hundreds of little yellow marbles appeared in the water.

"What is that?" I asked.

"Crocodile eyes," he said.

Above me were snakes that could eat a full-grown person with one swallow. Below me were man-eating fish. All that separated me from hundreds of crocodiles was a small canoe. With four people in the canoe, water lapped over the sides if we leaned too far to the left or right. Suddenly I realized that I was in for the adventure of a lifetime. Either that, or I was going to be fish food before the night was out.

Just when I thought I might be in over my head, the guide shimmied to the end of the canoe. He reached in like a snake striking a toad and flipped something into the boat. It landed with a thud at my feet.

It was a baby croc!

Have you ever found yourself following someone only to realize you were in over your head?

Emma did.

"You're never any fun," Hannah said. She put her hand on her hip and held out the keys. "What's the big deal?"

"I'll call my dad to pick me up. I'm not going."

It seemed like she was always the one saying no. She loved to have fun like anyone else, but Hannah's and her definition of fun often clashed.

Emma had found out what it meant to know God, and it was changing everything. Reading her Bible wasn't a chore because she knew she was hearing from God. Praying was a safe place where she could talk to God about everything. Her faith was real and alive, but sometimes that presented problems.

Like now.

"Just follow me. It will be fun!" Hannah made that face, the one that was supposed to make Emma feel sorry for her.

Follow me. That was a message that Emma heard every day. Dress the way I dress. Be the size I say you should be. Hang out with the people who matter.

But there was only one person Emma wanted to follow and that was Christ.

"I'll call my dad," Emma said again. The last time she climbed in a car with Hannah and her friends she was late for curfew. It was supposed to be a night at the movies, but Hannah picked up some guys she met at the mall the weekend before. They teased Emma about being too young to drive. One said she was hot and that he liked young girls. Hannah switched places with one of the guys and he drag raced another car, leaving sweaty black stripes on the asphalt.

"I guess my friends are right," Hannah said, breaking into Emma's thoughts.

"What do you mean?"

"This is what I get when I hang out with a fourteen-year-old."

Emma shook her head. She was five days away from her fifteenth birthday. They were in the same grade. Though Hannah was sixteen, she was only a year and a couple of months older. The truth is that Hannah had lied to her . . . again. When she invited her over, she said she had rented tons of movies. They planned to pop popcorn and eat ice cream while enjoying their all-night movie fest. There were no movies; worse, there were no parents.

They were out of town, and Hannah had told them she would be staying with Emma.

"Are you going to call your *daddy*?"

Emma nodded. "Yes," she said. "I can't go with you and I can't stay the night, but you are welcome to come with me. I have lots of movies at the house. It could be fun."

Hannah gave her a look of disgust. She threw the keys on the table. "Call your dad," she said, "but don't count on spending any more time with me after this weekend."

HEART CHECK

Everyone follows someone or something. Who or what do you follow?

Emma made the phone call. She was grateful that Hannah made the decision to end the friendship; it saved her from having to do it herself.

Emma's world is no different than yours. Your world is a noisy and chaotic place. Messages, standards, and expectations are blaring from so many different directions. These message bearers—the media, your friends, your teachers, your youth pastor, pop culture icons, authority figures, music, commercials, magazines, and more—blast at you, and chances are you don't stop often to sort through the messages. Every day these messages tell you what to do, what to wear, who to admire, and even what to think.

You've probably often felt inadequate, that there's no way you can live up to what's demanded of you. Honestly, how could you ever measure up?

Being a follower gets you in trouble when following takes you down the wrong road. Following Christ is a very different journey. It's an exploration of your true self. It's discovering the depths of a be-everywhere, know-everything God. It's hiking up and down paths you might never have encountered if not tracking after destiny.

Christ asks us to follow him. Let's see exactly what that means, both in Bible times and today.

Dropping and Following 1: You Respond to the Call

Jewish boys studied the Torah from the time they were young. Their teachers were Rabbis. Rabbis were highly respected scholars, almost like celebrities in the Jewish culture. They watched each of the students to see who excelled in their studies. After promising students memorized the entire Torah, a Rabbi might approach them individually.

"Follow me," he would say.

The student immediately picked up his books and followed the teacher. He ate with him. He slept nearby. He studied and learned from him. Being asked to follow a Rabbi was a high honor, a once-in-a-lifetime opportunity, and this opportunity just came Levi's way.

> After these things He went out and saw a tax collector named Levi, sitting at the tax office. And He said to him, "Follow Me." So he left all, rose up, and followed Him. (Luke 5:27–28 NKJV)

Levi had two names. One was Matthew.

He was a tax collector and despised by the people in the community. One reason was that tax collectors in that time were feared. They didn't make a lot of money, but they had a great deal of power, so they collected taxes for the government and then cheated the people to earn extra money for themselves. If the people didn't pay, the tax collectors had the power to make their lives miserable. The second reason that Matthew was despised was because of his heritage. The name Levi was a very special name. It was the name of the tribe of Israel that served God as priests throughout every generation.

Levi meant "set apart." Names held great significance in that culture. Matthew, a.k.a. Levi, was not only missing his calling, he was cheating his own people.

Matthew was hanging around the tax collector's booth when

Jesus approached him. Everyone in the community was talking about this teacher named Jesus. He was a Rabbi like no other. He taught in the temple, speaking deep truth about faith. He performed miracles. Some said the sky opened and God himself pronounced that this was the long-awaited Messiah. When Jesus stopped at the booth, Matthew might have expected condemnation from the Rabbi, but what he received was very different. Jesus spoke two simple life-altering words:

"Follow me."

Matthew immediately left his profession and everything behind to follow Jesus. The Jewish man was offered an opportunity he couldn't pass up. Somehow, some way, the Rabbi saw something in him that Matthew couldn't see for himself.

Did this encounter change Matthew? Absolutely. Matthew lived up to his name. He served as one of Jesus' twelve disciples. He ate with him. He slept nearby. He sat at Jesus' feet and learned from the greatest teacher on earth and in heaven. Eventually he wrote the book of Matthew, a gospel that continues to impact believers today. He became one of the respected founders of a faith that would change millions of people over thousands of years. This tax collector went on to find destiny as he followed in the footsteps of the Rabbi.

INTO ME SEE

Have I answered the call to follow Christ?

Jesus sees something in you. He knows your name. He knows your destiny. Following him means that you accept his call to walk with him for the rest of your life, to become a life-long learner of the faith. It means that you will discover your purpose and impact others because you answered the call of the Rabbi.

Dropping and Following 2: You Discover Your True Identity

Watch a fashion trend hit the magazines and stores and soon everyone is wearing the new look. Not me, you say! I'm a rebel. It's funny, but many people who proclaim that they are rebels end up looking like every other rebel.

The cool thing is that your faith has little to do with fashion. Yes, there are elements of modesty, but faith is a heart issue. People make assumptions on some of the strangest things—like how spiritual you are based on the length of your hair or whether you have piercings or even how you worship, but God looks deeper than that. He's checking out the cardio system of believers. He wants to know where your heart is.

Did you know that God has X-ray vision?

> Looks aren't everything. . . . GOD judges persons differently than humans do. Men and women look at the face; GOD looks into the heart. (1 Sam. 16:7)

Originality in your faith is finding out what God wants from you. He's examining your heart for motivation, for desire, for hunger, for willingness to hear and obey what he is saying.

Your identity has little to do with your exterior. It's hard to imagine, but one day you will lose your hair or maybe have hair show up in your ears! You'll invest in wrinkle cream. That's just life. But the inside of you can only get better and stronger and wiser if you choose to follow Christ. Following him is an entirely different path than hanging out at church two days a week. It's a daily walk with God. You eat with him. You talk with him. You stay near your faith, no matter where you are or what circumstances surround you. Finding your true identity means you are much more than someone who simply attends church. You are a modern-day disciple of Christ.

You are called to minister to a very diverse world. That ministry might be living as an example. It might be helping with children's church. It might be visiting the sick in the hospital or helping with a hospice for AIDS patients.

Your generation is not afraid to bust out of the church pews to take the good news to the people who don't know Christ. In a sense, you are repeating the invitation of Jesus, asking the Matthews of this world, "Do you want to follow Jesus? Do you want to join us in this adventure of destiny?"

INTO ME SEE

Do I identify myself as a disciple of Christ?

Dropping and Following 3: Your Faith Impacts Others

Across the world teenagers are making a difference. Teens work in the hot sun as they build homes with Habitat for Humanity. Others raise funds to travel with organizations such as Teen Mania and YWAM (Youth With a Mission) to build homes and to share the gospel in other nations. They volunteer in their churches, lead worship, set up for service, and pray for their friends.

In my home church Ashley leads worship. She is fourteen. She writes songs, and her heartbeat is to lead teenagers to praise God. She will soon record her own CD.

Drew is a football player who is tough on the field. He used to have a reputation as a fighter, but God impacted his life. Now he reaches out to younger teens in the youth group, making them feel at home. His presence is protective and welcoming.

Bonnie feels called to pray for others. Hailey is kind. Tyson is a shy guy who is bold in his relationship with God. Glorianna is gentle with others. Jill is a backup worship leader and sings with her best friend, Ashley.

INTO ME SEE

What is God calling me to do right now?

Serving others puts your faith in action. Many believers live their whole life and miss this exciting aspect of following Christ.

When Jesus began his ministry, he shocked people as he wrapped a towel around his waist and knelt to wash dirty feet, a job reserved for a servant.

Jesus reflected the character of God. Though he was a king in heaven, he served on earth.

> Those who oppress the poor insult their Maker, but those who are kind to the needy honor him. (Prov. 14:31 NRSV)

Following Christ means that you become a world changer through serving others. We'll talk more about that in the next chapter, but first you will take the next five days to define what it means to you to walk in the dust of the Rabbi.

Crucial Question: Does God Choose Me?
Real Scripture: 1 Samuel 16:1–13

When Samuel arrived at the house, Jessie's sons lined up like an NFL team. They were handsome and strong. When the oldest, Eliab, stood in front of Samuel, a conversation something like this kicked in between God and Samuel:

"Surely, this is God's anointed," Samuel said, checking out the biceps and rugged good looks of the tall, handsome eldest son.

"Look again," God said. "Are you seeing him like I do?"

"Hmm," Samuel said. "He looks like king material to me!"

"Stop looking at his appearance and his muscles. I didn't choose this guy. Don't you know by now that I don't care what's on the outside? I've looked at his heart, and he's not my choice."

One by one, Samuel went through all the brothers. Nada. Zilch. Not happening today. God flicked away the choices like flies.

"Okay, God. What now? We've been through all the brothers and there's no one left."

"Not true. Ask if there is another son."

There was. David was in the pasture at that moment. Samuel instructed Jesse to call his youngest son in from the fields. When the boy finally stood in front of the prophet, God gave a thumbs up.

"This is the one. I see his heart, and he's the next king."

"But Lord, did you notice that he's a boy. Are you sure you don't want to take another look at the older brothers?"

"I'm sure, Samuel. Anoint him."

Then Samuel took the horn of oil and anointed him in the midst of his brothers; and the Spirit of the LORD came upon David from that day forward. (1 Sam. 16:13 NKJV)

Making It Real

When Samuel anointed David, it was symbolic; but more than that it was spiritual. Something happened when the drops of anointing oil fell from the bottle and ran down over his head and down his shoulders. David assumed his true identity.

Are you waiting for people to give you the green light of acceptance? If so, you might get stuck in traffic for a long time. It's great if you are strong or beautiful. It's awesome if you are loved and accepted by your friends. But those things are not what God sees. He's looking at your heart. He sees the anointing on your life.

Do you ever let people keep you from stepping up as a man or woman of God?

_____

_____

_____

Talking with God

Anoint me, God. Pour out your Holy Spirit on my life. Drench me with purpose and calling. Help me to focus on my character, on courage, and to offer you a heart willing to serve.

DEVO DAY 2

Crucial Question: Which Message Do I Follow?
Real Scripture: Philippians 4

Maddee stood in front of the mirror and pinched her waistline.

"Gross!"

She sat on the edge of the bed and flipped through the fashion magazine. She already had a couple of the pieces in her wardrobe. If she bought a fun pair of shoes and some funky accessories, she'd have the perfect outfit.

"Maddee, it's dinner time."

The voice filtered up the stairs and Maddee groaned. She didn't know if she could continue to deceive her parents. It started when a friend lost ten pounds in one week. She looked great. She shared her secret with Maddee, who started her own weight loss program the next day. Maddee lost two pounds and then three more. At this rate she'd be perfect in a couple of weeks.

"Maddee!" Her mom stood in the doorway. "Are you coming to eat?"

Maddee set the magazine down. "Umm, I ate a huge snack after school."

This was the truth, at least part of it. She didn't tell her what she did after she was through eating.

Her mother frowned. They were close and Maddee knew that her mom was suspicious. "Baby, I want you to come and at least sit with us during dinner. Okay?"

Maddee nodded. She glanced in the mirror before she started down the stairs. The five lost pounds looked good, but the pain of lying to her mom was ugly.

Making It Real

There is a lot of pressure to have a certain image and to fit in. How do you know which message is the right one for you?

> Summing it all up, friends, I'd say you'll do best by filling your minds and meditating on things true, noble, reputable, authentic, compelling, gracious—the best, not the worst; the beautiful, not the ugly; things to praise, not things to curse. (Phil. 4:8)

As believers, it is vital that you unmask the messages you hear. Look at the heart of it. Is it asking you to harm your body? Is it saying that outward appearance is all that matters? Is it honorable? Is it real? There's nothing wrong with having fun with fashion, but if the message isn't true or honorable, then it's not a message to live by. If it's shallow and lacks character, why buy into it?

Ask God to help you judge the messages you hear before embracing them as truth.

Think about one message you hear from your culture, your friends, or the media. Using Philippians 4:8, unmask the message. What is it really saying?

_____

_____

_____

Talking with God

Lord, I'm swamped with voices in my ear telling me who to be, what to do, and how to live. Shut them all down, God, and help me to filter out the cultural messages that paint a bull's eye on my back and don't have my best interests at heart. Thank you for speaking to me. I'm listening!

DEVO DAY 3

Crucial Question: Am I Following the Rabbi?
Real Scripture: Luke 5:17–31

Some religious guys totally missed the fact that a paralyzed man was walking around after Jesus healed him. Instead, they were looking for a debate.

> And the scribes and the Pharisees began to reason, saying, "Who is this who speaks blasphemies? Who can forgive sins but God alone?" (Luke 5:21 NKJV)

The scribes were writers who painfully wrote down every single letter of every word of Scripture by hand. They knew about the prophecies. The Pharisees were teachers of the Law. But all the knowledge in the world was useless because they chose rules and tradition over a relationship with Jesus. They were blind to what they were missing.

Let's compare that to Matthew's story. When Jesus approached him, he became a follower of Christ that day. He wasn't trying to debate Jesus. He was so excited that he called all of his friends and held a big dinner party to honor Jesus.

Each of his friends had an opportunity to follow Jesus. Some chose religion. Matthew chose relationship.

Making It Real

Charity bent a finger for each trait.

"I never miss church. I read my Bible every night. I've never missed a mission trip. I don't drink. I don't go to parties. I even carry my Bible to school."

The problem with Charity's list was that it was self-righteous. She had forgotten she was a sinner saved by grace. If life didn't go the way she planned, she held up her list and reminded God that she was doing her part, so he better perform his end of the deal. She forgot that if he never did another thing, his sacrifice and his unconditional love were enough.

Think about it. What does it mean to have a Pharisaical attitude? How does that affect you as a follower of Christ?

_____

_____

_____

Talking with God

Lord, I'm opening up my heart, mind, and soul to you. Flash your revealing light on the deepest part of me and let me see what you see. If I'm blind to the miracle of being a child of God, expose it. If I'm religious but lack humility and thankfulness, point it out. Wash it out. Cleanse me. Get rid of it so I can start fresh.

DEVO DAY 4

Crucial Question: Do I Have a Servant's Heart?
Real Scripture: Acts 6:1–7

"Hey Colby, do you want to give to the hurricane relief fund?"

Colby darted around Brandon. "Nope. Giving isn't my spiritual gift. I'm a teacher. If anyone needs a lesson, I'm your guy."

Brandon sighed. He walked toward Jessie and Aaron. He held up the offering bucket. "We're sending an offering to help the evacuees who were hit by the hurricane. Do you have anything you can give? A dollar? Fifty cents? Anything will help."

"Sorry, I don't have any cash on me right now. Catch me later," Jessie said.

Aaron took a drink of soda and then set it down. "According to my D-teacher [discipleship teacher], I'm an administrator. Put me in charge of the details and I'll crack hardheads like Jesse here into giving you some cash."

"I'd rather you just give a dollar or two."

"Sorry, that's your job."

Brandon shook his head at the two bucks sitting in the bottom of the bucket. It wasn't worth the postage.

While the story above may seem ridiculous, it's a picture of *apathy*. That's a word that means that you don't care. If it doesn't affect your world, why bother? If it's not your gifting, then it must be someone else's problem. If it's not in your neighborhood, then it's someone else's mess to clean up. We are so bombarded with images of war and poverty and violence that it's almost numbing.

That can create apathetic believers.

Making It Real

Stephen was asked if he would serve food to the widows. This was considered a menial task. This man of respect and honor could have said, "Give this job to someone else!" but instead he served the widows with compassion.

Knowing your spiritual gift is important, but just because your spiritual gift is administration doesn't mean you can't also be a giver. The natural disaster my not have hit your family, but it devastated someone else's family. If you were hit by a hurricane, would you be grateful for contributions, no matter how small?

This isn't a guilt trip. It's an opportunity to serve and make an impact with your faith. Ask God today to give you a servant's heart.

What do you think it means to have a servant's heart?

_____

_____

_____

Talking with God

Father, I don't want to be apathetic. When I care, my world will see you inside of me. Help me today to have a servant's heart. I'm not big enough to change my world by myself, but I can be obedient in the small things.

Crucial Question: Do I Call Myself a Disciple?
Memory Verse: Luke 14:27

I pray that you now see yourself as a modern-day disciple. That's a very different role than just hanging out in a pew. It's important that you count the cost of being a disciple. It means that you keep your faith nearby and that it affects your choices, but it also means that you've stepped out of the religious box into a relationship with your Savior. After you answer the questions below, take a moment and journal your thoughts about this phase in your journey. Invite the Holy Spirit to assist you as you write, asking him to reveal even deeper truth.

_____

_____

_____

Luke 14:27–33 talks about counting the cost of following Christ. What does that mean to you?

_____

_____

_____

When a Rabbi chose a student, the student literally followed in his footsteps so closely that he was covered by the dust of the Rabbi's steps as he walked. How does that apply to your relationship with Christ?

_____

_____

_____

Write down one message for each numbered question:

1. Image: The cultural versus biblical message is:

_____

_____

_____

2. Sex: The cultural versus biblical message is:

_____

_____

_____

3. Relationships: The cultural versus biblical message is:

_____

_____

_____

4. Christianity: The cultural versus biblical message is:

_____

_____

_____

5. Family: The cultural versus biblical message is:

_____

_____

_____

Talking with God

Cover me in your dust, Rabbi. Take me higher and deeper and further than I can go on my own. Thank you for choosing me, God. I will follow you.

6

Becoming a World Changer

[REAL QUOTE]

I don't want to be like anyone else. I want the things of the spirit. I want his desire to be my desire. I want to listen to God and obey. I don't want to hold anything back. I put my confidence in him as he molds me, makes me, uses me, breaks me, stretches me.

—Bonnie W., age 16

If the ground opened up and swallowed me whole, my shouts of relief would have echoed. I was skinny and the tap, tap, tap of my knees danced in sync with the whoosh, whoosh, whoosh of my heart.

"Open your Bibles to Revelations 1," I said. I couldn't help but notice the look of apprehension on my youth pastor's face.

When he asked me to speak, I said yes and then second-guessed myself all the way home. I was only fifteen years old. What did I know about speaking? I was a new Christian. I loved reading the Bible and was so hungry to know more, but speaking?

I spent the next week trying to decide what to share. I wasn't sure where to begin, so I let the Bible fall open. (I was a baby

Christian, so give me some slack.) It landed on Revelations. For the next few days I read about end times and prophecy until my head swirled. I underlined and cross-referenced and wrote long, laborious notes. And that night when I finished speaking, I was relieved to get off the stage.

What do you do when you feel God calling you to rev your faith to a higher level? What do you do when you want to impact your world and you're a teen?

Josiah decided to find the answer to those questions.

Josiah grabbed his buddies and they prayed quickly. "God, show us what to do. Help us reach a world for you."

The three partners of Encore Productions stood backstage and watched as the crowd went crazy. Josiah signaled to the guys in the band.

"You'll follow these guys," he said to the lead singer. "Are you ready?"

"Yeah," he said. He hesitated. "Josiah, are you sure this is the right place for our music?"

Josiah nodded. This was what made Encore Productions different than any other Christian agency. It was his dream to put Christian music where it was needed most. He didn't want to sing about God only to Christians. It was his hope to share a message through music in avenues where Christians didn't hang out. He wanted to be light in a world looking for hope.

Josiah was only sixteen, but music was part of his life since he was a kid. He played in every kind of band. He could play the guitar, the piano, and the drums. He wrote music. But his true love was finding gigs for bands. It started out as a hobby, but now it was a dream come true. His parents and grandparents backed him financially. Two members of his old band threw in their savings and helped him with the details. He planned to go to college and get a dual degree in business management and music. It wasn't Bible school, but it was definitely ministry. It was right where God wanted him.

When he first approached the organizers of the huge music fest, they shot him down. His company was unknown. He was still in high school. The organizer didn't take him seriously. Josiah prayed and asked for direction. He printed out his favorite Scripture from 1 Timothy and put it on his computer where he could see it every day:

Let no one despise your youth, but be an example. (4:12 NKJV)

Josiah sent over some of the best music from one of the most promising bands. He received a phone call later that day from the head guy. He told Josiah that he really liked the style of the band. Josiah almost danced when he found out the band would be one of three local bands opening for the main attraction!

"Five minutes," the backstage director shouted, interrupting Josiah's thoughts.

The backstage crew member gave a hand signal to Josiah.

"Time! Ready guys?"

The band ran out on stage and launched into the music. It was sweet. The crowd roared. They threw people around the crowd and danced to the music. The lead singer slowed it down and sang one more song.

"Hey dude, that's a religious song," someone from the crowd shouted.

"Sing something else," another said.

Someone threw a can of beer onto the stage and it exploded.

The lead singer looked at Josiah with panic.

"Finish the song," Josiah mouthed.

The band finished the song. It was Josiah's favorite.

Reaching for something I don't know the name
Finding you faithful, it's your claim to fame

You draw me deeper and higher each day
I'll follow you Jesus, you've shown me the way.

HEART CHECK

Intimacy with God reveals opportunities to impact your world.

The crowd was quiet. One person started clapping. Others joined in and shouted wildly as they chanted the name of the band, calling out for one more tune. The bass player ripped into the next song and the lead singer grabbed the mike and belted out their final song. Backstage, Josiah couldn't help but smile.

He was in the right place at the right time, and it felt amazing.

Making It Real

Intimacy with God isn't just about knowing him, it's also about responding to his call. Stepping out in ministry is a step of faith. The lights may shine your way as showers of compliments fall at your feet. You might skid into a wall as you encounter roadblocks.

INTO ME SEE

Are you willing to follow Jesus and go where he takes you?

Let's go all the way back to chapter 1. What is God calling you to do? To believe in him. It's that simple and yet that life-changing. When you believe in God, you follow him. You obey and follow through as he presents opportunities for ministry.

A recent stat said that 83 percent of people would go to church if someone would only ask. And since most churches in this country have more than a few empty seats, this raises the question, "Why aren't we asking?"

Why do we miss opportunities to present Christ and change the world?

Reason 1: You Don't Know What to Do

I celebrated my fourteenth year as a cancer survivor this year. I took out a shoebox filled with notes and cards that I received during that time. Many of them were from teens. I sat up for hours reading those cards and notes. Many of them were funny and I laughed all over again. Some were so thoughtful that I wiped away tears. I remembered how teens made me signs and hung them in my hospital room after I had surgery. I kept all of them and they still encourage me.

Those cards and letters were a gift of encouragement.

> God's various gifts are handed out everywhere; but they all originate in God's Spirit. God's various ministries are carried out everywhere; but they all originate in God's Spirit. God's various expressions of power are in action everywhere; but God himself is behind it all. Each person is given something to do that shows who God is: Everyone gets in on it, everyone benefits. All kinds of things are handed out by the Spirit, and to all kinds of people! (1 Cor. 12:4–7)

Making It Real

Ministry is acting as the hands and feet of Christ.

You might not think that sending a get-well card to someone is a big deal, but every one of the notes I received helped me as I sought healing for my body. They helped me be strong in a time when I was in a battle for my life. I knew that there were teens who were fighting for me in prayer.

If you love to invite people over and make cool deserts, you might have the gift of hospitality. You make people feel comfortable. You would be awesome as a greeter in your youth group! You have the gift to make people feel welcome and that they belong.

That's ministry!

Grow your talents. Teaching is the gift God has placed inside of me, but did I mention I bombed my first speaking engagement? Here's what I didn't tell you earlier.

I spoke that night for almost forty-five minutes. I lost my audience. A faithful friend or two tried to hang in there, but even friendship can only go so far. Drops of perspiration glistened on my youth pastor's forehead as he watched teenagers trying to stay awake. I didn't know how to end my sermon, so I stopped in mid-sentence and said, "I'm done."

My youth pastor stepped up to the podium. "Thanks, Suz," he said. "Umm, nice job on the book of Revelation."

In the beginning I was awful because I tried to teach one of the most difficult and intricate books of the Bible. An already written Bible study or devotional would have been a much wiser choice.

But I didn't know!

This is the good news: my failure didn't stop God's plan or gifting in my life. Sometimes when we make a mistake in ministry, we give up too soon. If it's a passion, if it's something that you love and feel called to do, then it is worth developing. Just like a seed, you plant it and water it and watch it grow. It gets stronger and pushes roots down in the soil. This takes time. It means that you seek out people who are mature in that gift and learn from them. You pray over your gift and you practice it.

Reason 2: You Don't Feel Qualified

Nicole was abandoned by her parents when she was eleven years old. She lived with different friends for several weeks until the parents figured out that she was homeless and called the foster care system.

When I read Nicole's story I was amazed. She was eighteen and a talented writer. Her life had not been easy, but she felt strongly that she should share her story, and perhaps one day even write a book.

"I'm not sure if I'm good enough," she said.

I assured her that she had talent and her story was powerful. "Is that enough?"

"Writing is a tough industry. It's hard to break in and it takes a lot of patience and hard work, but Nicole, this is a gift. You've got to share it. Start working on your craft, but also trust that God can do things that you can't."

Nicole felt unequipped because of her background, her age, and by how hard the road to publishing is, but that doesn't make her story any less powerful.

She started writing devos about faith and trust and healing. Now she's writing her first book. She still feels unequipped at times, but someday her story will impact others.

It has already impacted me.

Making It Real

Can you say "limitations"? We all have them. Some of your limitations will become your strengths. I'm scared every time I speak, but that means that I get to trust God. My mantra is "Do It Afraid." When I step up and assume the role God has given me, I gain courage. He equips me!

I was sitting with a teen the other day. Her mom is bipolar and home isn't a fun place. She said, "I don't feel like I'm worthy of anything. I love God, but I don't feel like I do enough."

Her limitations were huge: a mom who was sick and verbally abusive. She wrestled with fear of never measuring up. At times, she doubted God because things weren't getting better. As I wrapped my arms around her I told her God was in control. Her limitations—as yuk as they were— were advantages in the hand of God. She

INTO ME SEE

Is it possible that God is calling me in spite of my limitations? Or maybe even because of them?

didn't need to try to do better, but just let God show her what he wanted. He had a plan and she was part of it. Not only that, but God wasn't afraid of her doubts.

INTO ME SEE

Hey, God chose me! Do I trust his judgment?

What about you? Do you focus on your limitations? Do you let them keep you from making a difference? God doesn't look at what the world is looking at. He's not searching for natural abilities or perfect circumstances. He's looking for a person of faith.

Is that you?

DEVO DAY 1

Crucial Question: Am I Gifted?
Real Scripture: 1 Corinthians 12

We are made to be one body—the Body of Christ—and we have a big job to do. A big job needs the attention of many people. When everyone works together, tapping into their spiritual gifts and working as a team, then the project can be completed.

What would happen if a natural disaster struck your church? If everybody used their natural and spiritual gifts, a well-organized army of people would come together to fix the problem.

The helpers would jump in with a hammer to start reconstructing the building. The administrators would organize teams. They would carry long to-do lists and know exactly who and what is needed for each job. Their efforts would help the project run smoothly from start to finish.

The givers would have a bake sale and car wash to raise funds for materials. The encouragers would boost morale. You'd hear them in the hallways: "Way to go, Joe! What a great job!" With such great teamwork, it wouldn't be long before the damage was repaired.

Making It Real

You are part of a team. What is your passion? What are your talents? These are great questions to ask as you uncover your spiritual gifts. Do you love reading the Bible and explaining Scripture to others? You might have the gift of teaching. Do people come to you when they are hurting? You might have the gift of mercy. When the pastor talks about giving to missions, is this exciting to you? You could have the gift of giving, or possibly the heart of a missionary.

There are diversities of gifts, but the same Spirit. There are differences of ministries, but the same Lord. And there are diversities of activities, but it is the same God who works all in all. (1 Cor. 12:4–6 NKJV)

What do you love to do? Serve? Lead? Pray? Visit the sick? Work with kids? Think about it and write down what a perfect day of ministry would look like.

_____

_____

_____

Talking with God

Compose a prayer to God and ask him to begin to reveal your spiritual gifts.

_____

_____

_____

DEVO DAY 2

Crucial Question: What if I Sink?
Real Scripture: Matthew 14:22–33

No wakeboard. No skis. Just two feet, a little bit of faith, and a whole lot of water. Peter stepped out of the boat and locked his eyes on Jesus. He performed two steps of the walk-on-water waltz until a gust of wind stepped on his toes. Suddenly the impossibility of what he was doing was very real.

> Peter got out of the boat, started walking on the water, and came toward Jesus. But when he noticed the strong wind, he became frightened, and beginning to sink, he cried out, "Lord, save me!" (Matt. 14:29–30 NRSV)

Peter was a fisherman, so he was aware of the dangers of drowning. But he was also a follower of Christ. He had a front-row seat as Jesus performed miracles, so when Peter heard the voice of God, he obeyed. Peter didn't want to just observe these miracles; he was ready to be a part of one. But 600 feet from solid land, doubt hit like a tidal wave. As the wind pushed him around and the fish nipped at the bottom of his feet, he wondered, "What in the world was I thinking?" The euphoria of walking on water was gone. His toes got wet, then his knees, then his waist. His step of faith suddenly felt like a nightmare.

Peter shouted out for Jesus to save him. The Master stretched out his hand and took hold of Peter. Peter found himself right in the middle of a teachable moment.

Making It Real

My favorite Olympic sport is couples ice-skating. I hold my breath when the guy takes the girl and spins her in the air over his head. The skaters make it look effortless, but the reality is that they hit the cold unforgiving slab of ice hundreds of times before they perfect a move. Their coach gives them direction, and they try again.

Just like the ice skaters, Peter was in training. When he doubted, the coach gave him instructions on how to get back up.

Have you ever taken a step of faith and it turned out different than you hoped? Did it discourage you from trying again? Many times, God will ask you to take that risk. Every time you obey and keep your eyes on him, you grow. If you bomb, he's there to help, but at least you listened to God.

If you take a step of faith and fail, what do you do? Do you give up? Do you try again? Maybe you just disappear into a witness protection program. Remember my Revelations teaching fiasco? What can you learn from my failure?

Talking with God

Lord, teach me through my mistakes and failures and successes. Thank you for being my spiritual coach. I place my destiny in your hands.

DEVO DAY 3

Crucial Question: Why Is Destiny Such a Big Deal?
Real Scripture: 2 Peter 3:8–17

Eternity isn't a popular word and yet it is a very real part of faith. Some describe heaven as cold—lots of gold with big thrones and angels floating around—but heaven is so much more than that. It's the ultimate definition of intimacy. It's a place God designed for those who love him.

God is patient. He's willing to wait as long as he can so that every person can come to know his love. Destiny is a big deal because you get to introduce others to God. You are part of that plan to help people find their way to faith.

Last year my testimony was picked up by an Internet newsletter service. The newsletter hit cyberspace and landed in about 40,000 in-boxes. People started forwarding it and my in-box was crammed every day. More than 250 e-mails came from South Africa. One person after another said things like:

- I read your story and I felt like it was a sign from God that he loved me.
- I'm sitting here at my desk and I'm crying. Is that God that I feel?
- My family is torn apart and I've lost hope. Will you pray for me?

I didn't realize how one story could impact so many, but it confirmed that people were looking for God, which is cool because God is reaching for them.

Making It Real

You might not see yourself as a world changer, but when you

stay in the game and play with all your heart, people are impacted
for eternity.

Three things happen when you share your faith.

1. People will accept Christ—winning situation.
2. People will reject Christ or maybe even you—not a winning
   situation.
3. You will plant a seed—winning situation.

That means that 66 percent of the time when you share your
faith you are in a winning situation. Most NBA players hope for a
40 percent average of success from the free-throw line. Now how
do your 2-out-of-3 odds sound to you?

Ask God for opportunities. You're not trying to make anyone
love God. It's the Holy Spirit who will do that. You just plant seeds
and let God gently water and shine light on them.

Are you a seed planter? Why or why not?

_____

_____

_____

Have you asked God to give you a burden for those who don't
know him?

_____

_____

_____

Talking with God

Let me be sensitive to the Holy Spirit. I ask for a renewed burden for the people around me who don't know your love.

DEVO DAY 4

Crucial Question: Can One Person Make a Difference?
Real Scripture: Isaiah 61

World changer. What a scary thought! How can one person make a difference? Have you read a newspaper lately? Have you listened to the problems facing our economy, our culture, our families?

Even the weather has gone haywire!

Ayee! This is just too much for one person, so this is the deal. I'm going to take care of me and no one else. That's my plan and I'm sticking to it. As long as I keep my nose clean and don't hurt anyone, I've contributed to a better world, or at least I haven't screwed anything up. Maybe it's not destiny, but at least it's doable.

Right?

> The Spirit of the Lord GOD is upon me,
> Because the LORD has anointed Me
> To preach good tidings to the poor;
> He has sent Me to heal the brokenhearted,
> To proclaim liberty to the captives,
> And the opening of the prison to those who are bound.
>
> (Isa. 61:1 NKJV)

Making It Real

In three years of ministry, Jesus left a lasting mark. He didn't live a safe life. He encountered mountains of resistance, but he also fulfilled the prophecy of Isaiah.

Want to change the world? Continue the work of Christ. Need a blueprint? Check out what I like to call the Destiny List.

Jesus changed the world by:

1. Preaching the Good News to the Poor

While Jesus fed the hungry and instructed the church to take care of the helpless, the word *poor* isn't limited to those who don't have money. Jesus shared good news with people who were poor in spirit. Everywhere he went Jesus shared this message: There's a better way! You don't have to earn God's love. I will pay the price for you. I will cover your sins.

2. Binding the Brokenhearted

Jesus healed sick bodies, but he also gave hope to people whose hearts were broken. He bandaged the open wounds by helping people to find their purpose as children of God. The Hebrew word for brokenhearted means "shattered soul." Do you know of anyone who is trying to fill the hole in his life with destructive choices? Do you know of someone who needs comfort? What can you do or say to show that you care?

3. Proclaiming Freedom for the Captives and Releasing Prisoners from the Darkness

These two phrases sound different, but have the same meaning. Jesus offered freedom from sin and bondage. The life change was the same as having the light turned on and eyes opened.

Being a slave to sin means that you are in darkness. When a baby is born, light floods his eyes. His senses are awakened to a world he has never experienced, but always knew was there. This describes a seeker who experiences Jesus for the first time.

Jesus can help people find freedom from sin, from addictions, from the past, from fear, from hurts, from a life that is based on shallow pursuits.

Pray for your friends and family. Believe for those you care about. Tell them and help them find the light.

How does this Destiny List help you to become a world changer?

_____

_____

_____

Talking with God

I can't change the whole world. In fact, God, I sometimes struggle to change myself. But I can introduce others to you. I can tell them what you've done in my life. I can live for you and let them see you inside of me.

Crucial Question: Am I Ready to Step into Destiny?
Memory Verses: John 4:28–42

You'll finish this chapter by answering the questions below and
then journaling your thoughts about what it means to have a *Just
You and God* relationship.

What did you learn about *direction?* Does intimacy with God
help you find your way?

_____

_____

_____

What *decisions* did you make about trusting God? Trusting
yourself?

_____

_____

_____

What do *dilemmas* teach you about faith?

_____

_____

_____

How does *destiny* impact your relationship with God? With others?

_____

_____

_____

Read these Scripture verses: Luke 14:12–13; John 3:16; 4:35; and 13:34–35. What message do these verses share about destiny?

_____

_____

_____

Talking with God

Thank you for helping me carve out my relationship with you. Lord, you've helped me to focus on what is life-changing. You've opened my eyes to the joy of knowing you better every day. I've just begun this amazing relationship with you! I know you are faithful to complete the work you've begun in me. Help me to be faithful to follow your plan.

MY
JOURNAL

If a Scripture leaped out at you and made perfect sense, write it down. Let God know what's going on in your life. Tell him about the road bumps that are slowing you down and ask him to help. Ask him to celebrate with you as you take giant steps in your spiritual walk. Write your thoughts, poetry, and more. This is your space!

Part 1: Direction

Chapter 1: Detours and Shortcuts

_____

_____

_____

_____

_____

_____

_____

_____

_____

_____

_____

_____

_____

_____

_____

_____

_____

_____

_____

_____

_____

Chapter 2: Dependently Strong

_____

_____

_____

_____

_____

_____

_____

_____

_____

_____

_____

_____

_____

_____

_____

_____

_____

_____

_____

_____

_____

_____

_____

_____

Part 2: Decision

Chapter 3: You and God

Part 3: Dilemma

Chapter 4: Trusting God

_____

_____

_____

_____

_____

_____

_____

_____

_____

_____

_____

_____

_____

_____

_____

_____

_____

_____

_____

_____

_____

_____

_____

Part 4: Destiny

Chapter 5: Drop Your Nets and Follow Me

Chapter 6: Becoming a World Changer

_____

_____

_____

_____

_____

_____

_____

_____

_____

_____

_____

_____

_____

_____

_____

_____

_____

_____

_____

_____

_____

_____

_____

I'm so excited that you've allowed me to be a small part of your journey of faith. This is the first book in a series designed to take you deeper in your walk with God.

If you need prayer or have questions, I'd love to hear from you. I believe in you, and I believe in what God can do when you seek him.

—Suzanne

To contact Suzanne, e-mail her at tseller@kregel.com. If you love to write poetry, devos, or stories about your faith, visit Real Teen Faith online. We'd love to read your story and possibly share it with teens across the nation.

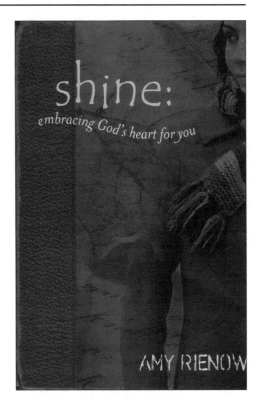

SHINE
Embracing God's Heart for You

"God created you to shine. Do you believe it?"

Most young women who've spent any time in the church know the
fundamental truths. They know who they are in Christ, and that they
should find their identity in Him rather than beauty, popularity, or
boys. Written for the young woman who has learned all the correct
answers in church but says, "so what?" this book shows her how to live
out the truth she's always known.

ISBN 10: 0-8254-3580-3 • ISBN 13: 978-0-8254-3580-5 • 160 pages

goGirl #1
REAL STUFF
A Survivor's Guide

Guy stuff... parent stuff... school stuff... sports stuff... clothes stuff... friend stuff—teen girls have a lot of "stuff" to deal with! And it can often seem like no one understands.

Enter Heather Jamison—someone who's been there, done that, and learned some valuable lessons along the way—someone who understands. She's written the essential survivor's guide because she knows just how hard dealing with all that "real stuff" can be. Heather covers the vital issues: rules, rags (clothes), and relationships. So, what's the bottom line? Heather wants girls to know that even though life is rough, no one has to do it alone!

> "This book helps bring an invaluable focus for teens. It's written with a fresh perspective from someone who understands the diversity of teens."
>
> —tobyMac

ISBN 10: 0-8254-2931-5 • ISBN 13: 978-0-8254-2931-6 • **160 pages**

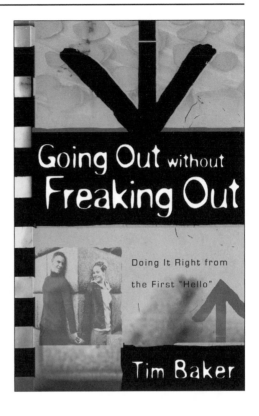

GOING OUT WITHOUT FREAKING OUT
Doing It Right from the First "Hello"

Dating—the mere mention of the word strikes people with both excitement and terror. Award-winning author and veteran youth leader Tim Baker lends fun-filled honesty to his personal and practical advice for how to navigate and how NOT to navigate the often treacherous terrain of dating. *Going Out Without Freaking Out* is based on biblical principles and offers stress-free tips on building relationships with the opposite sex, along with ideas for keeping God at the center of every stage of dating.

ISBN 10: 0-8254-2395-3 • ISBN 13: 978-0-8254-2395-6 • 160 pages